A TOOLKIT
FOR COLLEGE
PROFESSORS

A TOOLKIT
FOR COLLEGE
PROFESSORS

Jeffrey L. Buller
and
Robert E. Cipriano

ROWMAN & LITTLEFIELD
Lanham • Boulder • New York • London

Published by Rowman & Littlefield
A wholly owned subsidiary of The Rowman & Littlefield Publishing Group, Inc.
4501 Forbes Boulevard, Suite 200, Lanham, Maryland 20706
www.rowman.com

Unit A, Whitacre Mews, 26-34 Stannary Street, London SE 11 4AB

British Library Cataloguing in Publication Information Available

Library of Congress Cataloging-in-Publication Data Available

ISBN 978-1-4758-2084-3 (cloth)
ISBN 978-1-4758-2085-0 (pbk.)
ISBN 978-1-4758-2086-7 (e-book)

♾™ The paper used in this publication meets the minimum requirements
of American National Standard for Information Sciences—Permanence of
Paper for Printed Library Materials, ANSI/NISO Z39.48-1992.

Printed in the United States of America

This book is dedicated to our hardworking colleagues who serve as coordinators in the Kingdom of Saudi Arabia's Academic Leadership Center and consistently inspire others with their high achievements in faculty success: Saeed Al-Amoudi, Abdulaziz Barnawi, Yasser Fallatah, Mohammed Ba-Shammakh, Ali Al-Shaikhi, Usamah Al-Mubaiyedh, Samir Alghadhban, Wail Mousa, and Said Ali Al-Garni.

CONTENTS

ACKNOWLEDGMENTS

The authors are grateful to Patricia Mosto and Dianne Dorland whose *A Toolkit for Deans* provided a model for our previous work, *A Toolkit for Department Chairs*, as well as the current volume. In addition, we are grateful to Sandy Ogden and Selene Vazquez for their editorial assistance, and to the hundreds of participants in our workshops over the years with whom we field-tested many of these case studies.

We would like to thank our editor, Tom Koerner, and our associate editor, Carlie Wall, for their support throughout this project. The efficiency with which they understand our vague concepts for a book and help us turn them into something that college professors will actually find useful is nothing short of amazing.

Finally, we want to recognize our spouses, Sandra and Raffaela, who offer us endless encouragement, miss us when we're away conducting workshops somewhere on the other side of the globe, and tolerate our bad jokes.

PREFACE

Being a college professor can be a confusing job. People usually enter this profession because they were excellent students who conducted research that was successful enough to earn them an advanced degree. And research, as we'll see, is certainly an important aspect of a faculty member's duties. But many college professors begin their work with little preparation in how to design a course, teach a class containing more than a hundred students, adapt that course to meet the needs of students who take it online, contribute to an accreditation self-study, chair a meeting effectively, resolve a dispute with a colleague, help a struggling student become more successful, or perform the dozens of other tasks that people just expect them to learn somewhere along the way. It's like entering a workshop with an empty toolkit.

Make no mistake about it: Graduate schools are recognizing the need to provide a better preparation for students who are seeking careers in higher education. As a result, they often come to their jobs with a much better skill set than did those of us who entered the profession thirty or forty years ago. But they still need additional tools in their toolkits, and this book has been designed to provide some of those tools.

Every college professor is different. Some enjoy the solitary thrill of devoting long hours to research projects that belong to them alone. Others prefer being part of a team where they can share ideas with others and together reach a more satisfactory conclusion than they could ever have reached on their own. The stereotypical college professor is just that: a stereotype. There's no single profile that embraces us all. College professors can be quiet and authoritative or boisterous and argumentative. They can see themselves primarily as teachers who perform research and service, researchers who also teach and serve, or public servants who teach and conduct research. They can be coldly intellectual or fiery and passionate. The only wrong type of college professor is one who is trying to be someone who he or she is not. The *best* college professors are those who let their unique talents and personalities come out through their own approaches to teaching, research, and service.

Very few experienced college professors ever say that, if given the chance, they would have chosen a different career. Very few experienced college professors ever say that they'd discourage their own children from entering this career. That's a completely different result from what you get if you'd pose that same question to doctors, lawyers, actors, and people in many other professions. Being a college professor puts you in daily contact with interesting people. It gives you a chance to help others achieve their dreams. It allows you to work with complex and interesting ideas. It really is more than just a career or even a profession; it's a way of life, a way of interacting with and understanding the world.

All it takes to begin the journey from being a good college professor to an excellent college professor is a few tools. So turn the page, and let's begin.

INTRODUCTION

When we were just starting out as college professors, we were talking to a professor at his retirement party. He was discussing the course he'd taught for more than thirty-five years and said, "The first few times I taught that class, it took a full year to cover the material. After about the tenth time I taught it, I found I could cover everything in a semester. During the last few, I covered the material by midterm and used the second half of the class to introduce the students to research methods. Now I imagine I could cover everything that needs to be covered in six weeks."

We were surprised by this remark, assuming that the more we learned, the more we'd want to teach our students and the longer that would take. As brand-new faculty members, we were all in favor of getting as much material into each course as possible, maintaining high standards, and teaching our students everything we knew ourselves. So, what was this faculty member's secret? Did he learn more effective ways of structuring the class? Did he discover that he could give fewer tests? Did he simply talk faster? Or did he, as we feared, lower his standards and just let the students get by with doing less?

When we asked him why he thought he was able to do in six weeks what had formerly taken an entire year, his answer was just as surprising as his original statement: "I just learned what's important."

We weren't quite sure what he meant at the time. But now, after more than thirty-five years in the classroom ourselves, we think we do. Experience as a college professor helps you identify what's really important in your teaching, research, and service; place a priority on these important activities; and not get distracted by less significant issues. Experience is a wonderful teacher.

Unfortunately, you can't wait until just before your retirement to gain all the experience you need in order to excel as a college professor. That's where A *Toolkit for College Professors* comes in. Case studies and scenarios provide a shortcut to the type of experience faculty members need. As you read each situation we present, we encourage you to ask yourself the following questions.

- What process did I use to decide how I'd handle this challenge?
- Do I seem to be reverting to the same two or three processes again and again even though the situations I'm reading about are very different?
- If I decided to change my tactics on the basis of one or more of the questions that followed the case study or scenario, what were the factors that led me to choose a different approach?
- Did the case study or scenario seem to suggest any fundamental values that are guiding me in making my decisions?
- If I were to develop a statement of my own philosophy of what being a college professor means, how could I incorporate some of the concepts I learned about the work of a faculty member from this case study or scenario?

Mixed in with all the case studies and scenarios, we've also provided some advice we've learned from our own experience as college professors. Like the professor whose retirement party we attended all those years ago, we distilled this advice into what we regard as truly the most important. As a result, each section of this book takes only a few minutes to read. In fact, the entire book has been constructed so as to be concise enough that you can easily work with it in the course of your busy schedule.

But concise doesn't mean simplistic. Give the discussions, case studies, and scenarios in this book the time and attention they deserve. For each case study, we've provided a resolution, and for each scenario we've provided an outcome. These resolutions and outcomes aren't designed to be the answers to all the questions each situation raises. In fact, none of the situations we describe has only one "solution." Real life isn't like that. Many of the problems we face have multiple possible solutions. Some have no solutions. What we've done is illustrate for you one possible way in which the case study or scenario could have played out. Compare the choices we describe to those you would have made yourself. Would the result possibly have been better by adopting the course of action you preferred? Would more complications have arisen? Did the decision we outlined fit your own personality and style as a faculty member?

We encourage you to discuss these case studies and scenarios with your colleagues. See if the way in which they would've handled the situation matches your own. Explore with them why they would have acted as they did and what those decisions might reveal about who they are as college professors.

We hope that *A Toolkit for College Professors* will be a valuable resource no matter whether you're using it as a textbook in a course on higher education, as a workbook in a faculty development program, as a guidebook at a professional conference, or as a book chosen for your own development that you read independently. However you use it, we think you'll find the advice we provide to be immediately practical and the situations we describe to be realistic enough to capture some of the complexity of a career as a college professor today.

As you make your own discoveries as a faculty member, we'd love to hear from you. In the meantime, congratulations on being part of the most wonderful community we can imagine: the community of scholars that includes professors at colleges and universities all over the world.

Jeffrey L. Buller
jbuller@atlasleadership.com
Jupiter, Florida

Robert E. Cipriano
rcipriano@atlasleadership.com
Madison, Connecticut

www.atlasleadership.com
July 1, 2015

I

TEACHING EFFECTIVELY IN THE CLASSROOM AND BEYOND

Learning is not a spectator sport. . . . [Students] must talk about what they are learning, write about it, relate it to past experiences, apply it to their daily lives. They must make what they learn part of themselves.

—A. W. Chickering and E. F. Gamson,
"Seven Principles for Good Practice in Undergraduate Education"

When most people think of college education, the image that probably comes to mind is that of a lone college professor lecturing on some arcane topic to an auditorium filled with several hundred students who are all busily writing down what they hear in their notebooks. The professor is probably either reading from or focused on a set of notes written many years before. If students are allowed to talk at all, they are limited to asking a few questions at the end of the class, most of which the professor will answer curtly or with a disparaging comment that begins with the phrase, "If you had actually read the assignment."

Movies and television programs still reinforce this depressing stereotype, an image that's all the more unfortunate for at least three very important reasons.

1. We've known for decades that lecturing, particularly to large groups where students can easily become disengaged and dismiss what they find uninteresting as insignificant, is one of the least effective ways for college professors to teach.
2. Prospective students who could benefit from a rigorous college education may choose to forego that opportunity because, encountering this cliché so often in popular entertainment, they assume that the modern university has little to offer them.
3. Even though higher education has advanced significantly in its understanding of how people learn and how best to promote the development of critical-thinking skills, some college professors— perhaps even *many* college professors— do still actually teach this way.

In other words, despite all we know about the importance of promoting active learning, the lecture—perhaps enhanced with a few colorful images or combined with a PowerPoint presentation—is alive and well. In many college classrooms, you'll find instructors transmitting facts and figures instead of developing insight and wisdom, talking in a monologue throughout nearly the entire class period, and repeating what's in the textbook instead of using the text as a foundation to promote higher order thinking skills. Why?

There are many reasons for the survival of the lecture, all of them compelling but none of them satisfactory.

- We teach the way that we were taught and, if we went to college and experienced lectures ourselves, we're more likely to continue this practice with our own students.
- Creating active learning experiences is extremely time-intensive, and we often find our days consumed by the need to keep up with our research, serve on endless committees, and complete all the dozens of other tasks that our deans and chairs expect of us.
- We often feel that we have to cover a certain amount of material in each class. In certain classes, we don't even write our own syllabi; the required content of the course is set by the discipline as a whole. If we don't get through all the objectives that have been set,

we may be considered to have failed in one of our responsibilities. Lecturing is simply faster than student-centered course activities.

- We may be experts in disciplinary *content*, although not in effective *pedagogy*. As a result, we may feel uncomfortable adopting new teaching techniques, particularly when the only chance we would get to practice them would be in the actual courses.

- The pressure on administrators to reduce the cost of college and increase faculty productivity means that massive course sections, particularly at the introductory and intermediate levels, are now the norm at many schools. Even if we think it might be interesting to incorporate active learning techniques in smaller course sections, we may feel overwhelmed by the prospect of monitoring these activities when they involve more than three hundred students at once.

Fortunately we have an opportunity to learn from one another and discover innovative ways of overcoming these obstacles. Throughout the 2014–2015 academic year, the authors surveyed 668 college professors each month to learn more about the ways in which they performed the various aspects of their jobs and to receive insights into what they discovered along their professional journeys. The surveys included faculty members at all kinds of institutions—large and small, public and private, comprehensive in mission and focused on particular disciplines—and provided a broad cross section of opinions about what college professors do, believe, and aspire to.

It turns out that a full 71 percent of the faculty members the authors surveyed could identify at least one active learning strategy that they used regularly. (Our survey defined *regular use* as a technique that the professor adopted at least once every two or three weeks). Those responding to the survey also identified the techniques they found most successful, and their suggestions provided a number of useful tools for every college professor's toolkit.

Almost half, 47.1 percent, had adopted the strategy known as **Think-Pair-Share**, in which students ponder the answer to a question and then share their thoughts with a neighbor who also provides his or her own perspective.

Just over one-third, 35.3 percent, engaged in one or more of the following activities:

- **Case Studies**, which require students to examine real or hypothetical situations and discuss how they would handle them
- **Problem-Based Learning**, in which the instructor poses a problem for the class to solve and, rather than offering the students a definitive solution, guides the students in applying their previous knowledge, material learned from the textbook, teamwork, and their own ingenuity in finding one or more possible solutions
- **Game-Based Learning**, in which students play carefully designed educational games that either teach or reinforce course material

Less than one-third, 29.4 percent, of the respondents to our survey used **One Minute Essays** or **Microthemes**, very brief essays that students complete at either the beginning or end of class on what they learned from the homework assignment, course discussion, or textbook.

Even fewer, 11.8 percent, adopted either or both of the following activities:

- **Jigsaw Groups**, a technique developed by Elliot Aronson in which a complex topic is divided into pieces that students examine and discuss in several subgroups. For example, students in a course on environmental policy might be assigned to different groups that explore various possible ways of dealing with an ecological disaster; we could call these groups the *strategy groups*. At the same time, one member from each group would also be assigned to a different group that specialized in one dimension of each solution: legislative challenges, cost factors, ethical issues, public health concerns, and so on; these would be the *issue groups*. When meeting in their strategy groups, students would be responsible for examining that particular strategy through the lens of the issue they were assigned. When meeting in their issue groups, students would be asked to compare the relative merits of the strategy they were assigned to all other strategies from the perspective of that specific issue.
- **Role Playing**, an activity in which students assume the identity of someone else and act in the way they imagine that person would act in a given situation

And a small number, 5.9 percent, of the college professors surveyed regularly engaged in one or both of the following techniques:

- **3-2-1**, in which students end a class by summarizing the three most important points that were covered in that session, two major aspects of the topic there wasn't time to talk about in class, and the one issue they're still most unclear about
- **Cooperative Small-Group Discussions**, in which students write down the most important concepts encountered in a homework chapter and bring their notations to class for small-group discussion

Many of the techniques these professors suggested fall under what's been called the *flipped classroom approach*, whereby students are responsible for learning facts, formulae, and other basic principles outside of class so that class time can be devoted to applying rather than introducing that material. The idea is not to transmit information in class and expect students to process it outside of class in their homework assignments, papers, and exam preparation. Instead, this approach is "flipped," so that information is acquired outside of class (from the textbook, websites, recorded lectures, and other sources) and then processed in class through the various activities our respondents highlighted.

Other strategies involve **co-teaching**, the pedagogical method whereby students are assigned the task of mastering a particular concept or unit and then teaching it to others. As you probably know from your own experience, you never really learn a concept well until you have to explain it effectively to someone else. Co-teaching thus involves the students directly in both their own educational success and that of others in the course.

With these tools for promoting active learning in our toolkits, it's now time to see how we might use them in our day-to-day work as college professors.

CASE STUDY 1.1: IT'S NOT JUST THE STUDENTS WHO CAN LEARN

One of your friends from graduate school is now teaching at a university not far from you. You've stayed in touch and, since you're both in the same stage of your career, sometimes contact one another for advice and support. One day your friend calls you to ask about a problem. It seems that your friend hasn't been satisfied with the ratings students have been providing on course evaluations for the last few semesters. As a result, your friend decides to distribute a strictly informal mock evaluation to this semester's students after only about a third of each course has elapsed.

The results are devastating. Students say that they're bored with the material in every class regardless of its topic or size. In one large course, the students say that they almost never do the reading, don't pay attention in class, wouldn't recommend it to their friends, and wish they hadn't taken it. Even in a small seminar class for advanced students that your friend thought was going very well, the students report that they're disengaged, thinking about switching to a different program, and annoyed that the course is required.

You're surprised to hear these results because, in graduate school, your friend was always energetic and personable. You would have guessed that your friend would be receiving awards for excellence in teaching, not course evaluations like the ones you just heard about.

Questions

1. Is there any general advice you think might be helpful to your friend?
2. Would your advice be any different if the large class were:
   a. taught in an auditorium?
   b. delivered online?
   c. taught partially in person and partially online (i.e., a *hybrid* course)?
   d. led by the professor twice a week and divided into discussion sections of twenty students each, led by graduate teaching assistants, once a week?
3. Would your advice be any different if the small seminar class were:
   a. an upper-division course for undergraduates?
   b. a course largely taken by master's degree students?
   c. one of the last courses taken by doctoral students before they began their dissertations?

4. How might your advice change depending on your friend's academic discipline? In other words, how might you tailor your advice to each of the following fields: the humanities, fine and performing arts, social and behavioral sciences, natural sciences, health professions, engineering, business administration, education, and architecture?

Resolution

You sympathize with your friend and lend your support, asking a few follow-up questions about the format in which the courses are being taught, the pedagogical techniques that are being used, and the timeline when the scores on student course evaluations began to decline. You learn that there appears to be a correlation between the start of the students' dissatisfaction with your friend's courses and an increased service obligation that has made your friend's workload far larger than it had been in the past. As a result, the large class has been taught primarily in a lecture format; your friend feels that there just hasn't been enough time to develop more innovative teaching strategies and says, "I already have the notes for the lectures. About all I have time to do is to go over them a few minutes before class begins and then present that day's set of concepts to the students." The seminar class, too, seems to have been suffering from a lack of preparation time, largely due to the increase in service assignments that your friend's chair and dean have imposed. Students appear to be picking up on the fact that your friend has not been fully prepared for certain discussions.

Your advice consists of two parts. The first part is a recommendation that your friend have a serious conversation with the department chair about the possibility of some relief from the number of committees and task forces that have been assigned recently. You encourage your friend to show the chair the result of the informal course evaluations that just came in, as well as the official student evaluations from the last few semesters. You advise your friend to point out how closely the decline in student ratings parallels the new committee assignments and to phrase the request for a service reduction in terms of how having more time to prepare for class would improve the students' educational experience.

The second part of your advice involves how your friend can re-place an over-reliance on lecturing with some more active learning techniques. "You don't have to invent it all yourself," you say. "There are lots of good resources that will save you preparation time even as you adopt approaches that promote increased student engagement. In addition to the various active learning techniques presented earlier in this chapter, you might also recommend the following resources to your friend:

- The website of the **Schreyer Institute for Teaching Excellence** at Pennsylvania State University, which includes a broad range of resources for promoting active learning in large classes, answers to frequently asked questions about how to be more effective in teaching these sections, and advice for working with teaching as-sistants. See www.schreyerinstitute.psu.edu/tools/alphasearch.aspx. The Schreyer Institute also provides access to resources that your friend can use in other classes, like the small seminar course. See www.schreyerinstitute.psu.edu/Tools.
- The website of the **Karen L. Smith Faculty Center for Teach-ing & Learning** at the University of Central Florida, which not only offers tips on how to be more effective in teaching large classes but also provides links to the websites of many other learn-ing centers at colleges and universities of all kinds. See www.fctl. ucf.edu/TeachingAndLearningResources/LearningEnvironments/ largeclass.php.
- *McKeachie's Teaching Tips* (Svinicki & McKeachie, 2014), the classic source used by generations of college teachers to improve their pedagogical techniques, which is regularly updated to remain relevant to the changing needs of today's college students
- John Bean's *Engaging Ideas* (2011), which contains a wealth of ideas for the use of writing assignments in all types of classes so as to increase student engagement and encourage active learning
- Dee Fink's *Creating Significant Learning Experiences* (2013), which builds on research about how people learn best as a way of developing approaches to promoting active learning in the college classroom

CASE STUDY 1.2: WHOSE FAULT IS IT?

You're teaching an introductory course in your discipline and, at first, everything seems to be going well. Attendance has been good. You've had a few assignments on which the students received the range of grades you'd ordinarily expect. While only a small percentage of the students have come to see you during your office hours, the rate of participation during class has been at or above the level you expected it to be.

Imagine your surprise, therefore, when every student in the class failed the first exam—not just *most* of the students, but every last one. And they didn't just miss a passing grade by a few points. Even the best exam paper was at least twenty-seven points lower than a passing grade on your institution's regular curve. You double-check the answer key; everything is correct. You go over the questions again; everything was covered both in class and in the textbook. In fact, many of these questions are slight variations of those you've used in the past without any problems.

Your first clue that something was different came as the students were turning in the exams. To describe their look as dazed would be an understatement. They seemed shocked, defeated, and overwhelmed. At first you merely attributed this reaction to test anxiety. Now you realize that the students could tell they weren't doing well and were not at all prepared for the exam you gave them. As you look over the range of grades again, you conclude that more than half the class cannot receive a higher grade than a C minus, even if they receive a perfect score on every other assignment and exam in the course.

You're at a loss about what to do about the situation. You could simply let the grades stand as they are, but that would mean that many students will fail the course and that many others will receive Cs and Ds. You could throw out the test entirely, but you're afraid you may be sending the message that there are no serious consequences for poor performance. You could curve the grades, but you feel uncomfortable about giving a student an A or B for answering fewer than half the questions correctly when early classes had performed so much better.

Of greatest concern, however, is that you can't quite determine what the problem was. Is this poor performance the fault of the students who perhaps didn't study as much as they should have? Is the fault yours because you somehow hadn't taught the material as well as you had in the past? Does the fault lie with the exam, which perhaps wasn't a good measure of what the students knew about the material? Without knowing the answers to these questions, you're afraid that you may have a similar problem in the future.

Questions

1. Suppose that today was the day on which you told the class you'd have their grades on this exam. What would you say to them?
2. Imagine that you consulted a trusted mentor in your discipline. How might you handle the situation if he or she said one of the following?
   a. "Oh, just let them suffer. You gave them every chance to succeed. They earned those failing grades. Sometimes you have to teach students that there's no one to bail them out when things go wrong."
   b. "Really? I know most of the students in your class. They're bright, and they work hard. I'm sure they didn't *all* deserve to fail."
   c. "That happened to me once. I just dropped that test and gave a make-up test the following week. Their grades all improved tremendously."
3. Would your approach be any different if the course were one of the following?
   a. A small section of twenty students
   b. A large section of 240 students
   c. An online course
   d. A lecture course in which the students met with you twice a week and then had discussion sections with teaching assistants once a week

Resolution

As you reflect on the situation, you conclude that there are several considerations that will guide you in how you deal with it. First, the students had done as well on their assignments as others in the past, suggesting that they were perfectly capable of learning the material. Second, the students hadn't taken one of your exams before, so it's possible that this particular class wasn't quite sure of what your expectations were. Third, since *every* student failed, you think it's highly unlikely that the students simply didn't study hard enough; if the test had been an accurate measure of their ability and preparation, at least one or two students would have passed. Fourth, although you're tempted simply to drop the test and offer a make-up exam, you feel this approach would put you too far behind on the syllabus.

Taking all these factors into account, you decide to say the following to the students on the day you return the graded exam papers. "I've got to tell you frankly that the grades on this exam were quite low. Perhaps the exam itself was too hard. Perhaps you didn't study enough or weren't clear about my expectations. Perhaps we were all just having a bad day. I can't be sure. I'm passing back the papers with the grades you earned, and I haven't adjusted or curved them at all. But here's what I'm going to do. We have our second exam in three weeks. I'm going to offer a number of review sessions the week of the test where we'll work together through questions similar to the ones on the exam. I strongly urge you to attend those sessions.

"If a student receives a grade on the second test that's at least one full letter grade higher than what he or she received on this first test, I'm going to reward that improvement. I'll drop the grade on the first exam and count the grade on the second exam twice. But remember: You have to get at least one full letter grade higher on that test or the grade you're getting today will stand. That's a pretty strong incentive to do your very best next time."

TEACHING PREFERENCES

As college professors, we have a really wonderful career. We get to work with important ideas. We have the luxury of getting paid to do many of the things we love. And we make a positive difference in the lives of many students. But that doesn't mean that we can just do whatever we want. Frequently the courses we're expected to teach are not the ones we'd choose at the times we'd choose in the format we'd choose.

As part of the same faculty survey we considered earlier, the authors presented participants with a list of nine common types of college courses and asked them to rank these courses from those they would most prefer to teach to those that they would rather avoid, if given the chance. As might be expected among groups as diverse as those taking the survey, the answers the authors received ranged widely. There were always people who said that the courses they enjoyed most were precisely those that others found least appealing.

Yet several clear patterns did emerge. Most professors said that their absolute favorite course to teach was a graduate seminar that included between twelve and twenty-five students (with 72.1 percent of respondents ranking it among their top three choices) or an upper-level course for the same number of undergraduates (with 61 percent of participants listing it among their top three choices).

As for formats that faculty members disliked, the most common answer was a section of an introductory undergraduate course that enrolled more than two hundred students. A vast majority, 94.3 percent, of the respondents said they'd prefer not to teach this class if it were a general education course for non-majors. Over three-fourths, 77.7 percent, said they wouldn't like to teach a large course section even if it was intended for majors in their field.

The other five options presented to participants in the survey all had a mix of admirers and detractors, as follows:

- 39.1 percent enjoyed supervising a graduate internship, practicum, or professional experience, while 33.2 percent said it was one of their least favorite ways to teach.
- 38.8 percent liked teaching a small to medium section (defined in the survey as enrolling between twenty-five and sixty students) of an introductory undergraduate course for majors, while 11 percent would prefer to avoid that format.
- 33.1 percent enjoyed giving lectures if the course were intended for graduate students, while 36.4 percent would rather avoid classes of this kind.
- 22.5 percent liked teaching a small to medium section (again defined as enrolling between twenty-five and sixty students) of an introduc-

tory undergraduate general education course for non-majors, while 27.7 percent rated that among their three least favorite formats.

- 22.1 percent of those surveyed found it enjoyable to teach an intermediate-level course (which the authors defined as a course students typically take in their sophomore or junior year) if it provided service to non-majors, while 5.5 percent ranked this type of class low.

What we can conclude from these results is that faculty members who wish to distinguish themselves as excellent teachers and at the same time fill a critical need at their institutions may want to develop their skills in teaching large courses. The results of the survey suggest that most of a faculty member's colleagues will probably prefer not to teach those classes and would be glad to be freed of this responsibility. With the budgets at most colleges and universities tightening (and with strong pressure from legislators, trustees, and parents to keep tuition costs controlled), the need for faculty members to teach large course sections is likely to continue. So, if a faculty member develops a reputation as a superstar at teaching classes with high enrollments, everyone benefits, and his or her reputation for excellence in teaching is all but assured.

Keep in mind, however, the advice we considered earlier in this chapter: Teaching a large class does not have to mean *lecturing* to a large class. Active learning is important, no matter what format a course is in. In fact, when participants in the survey were asked what advice they'd give to a new college professor about how to be an effective teacher, nearly all the answers participants gave fell into one of two categories.

- About two-thirds of respondents urged those just starting out in the profession to avoid lecturing as much as possible. As alternatives, they recommended case studies, group work, complex exercises, and the other forms of active learning we explored earlier.
- The remaining third of respondents encouraged their fellow faculty members to understand the needs of today's college students. As one participant put it, "Don't assume that students today are identical to students when you yourself were in school."

SCENARIO 1.1

As part of your course assignment, you teach an introductory class that regularly enrolls over two hundred students. You've been successful in incorporating a number of active learning strategies into this class, with one exception that's eluded you: activities that improve the students' skills in written communication. You believe that writing is important, and you haven't been pleased with the level of writing many students have demonstrated in your upper-level courses.

Last year you thought you'd discovered a solution. Once a week, your large course broke into a dozen discussion sessions of about twenty students each. You worked with the graduate teaching assistants who conducted those discussion sessions and devised a number of writing assignments, including a brief research paper, which the teaching assistants would grade. This year, however, severe budget cutbacks have eliminated teaching assistants from all courses. You'd like to continue to develop the students' proficiency in writing, but grading more than two hundred papers seems overwhelming.

Challenge Question:

Is there any way to keep a strong writing component in your course without creating a burden for you when you have to grade such a large number of assignments?

Scenario Outcome:

After discussing the situation with your mentor and others in your discipline, you decide that you have several options. First, you'll have students complete a "microtheme," a one-minute essay, roughly every other week. These short writing assignments can be graded very quickly: Students will receive an extra point on the next exam if they complete it and no points if they don't. You can look over this type of assignment very quickly and gain insights into where the students need additional help. For example, the prompts you'll use on these assignments will include such statements as "The one point about this unit that I wish I understood better is . . ."

SCENARIO 1.2

One of your courses enrolls more than three hundred students and has been assigned to a large auditorium. The configuration of the room will make break-out groups difficult, but you're resolved to be as creative as you can in developing active learning strategies that suit this challenging environment.

One difficulty that you face, however, is that you're required to adhere to a course syllabus that has set very ambitious goals for the amount of material that needs to be covered. You're not at liberty to change these course objectives, and you wouldn't want to even if you could: Some of the students in the course will be taking intermediate and advanced courses from you later, and you want to be sure that they're familiar with all the material required for this course.

Challenge Question:

How do you balance the need to cover such a large body of material with your own desire to promote active learning?

Scenario Outcome:

You decide that this course is tailor-made for the flipped classroom approach discussed earlier in this chapter. Although it requires a substantial investment of time, you devote an entire summer to making audio and video recordings of the material you ordinarily would have covered in your course lectures. Throughout the course, students listen to or watch these recordings as part of their regular homework assignments and then come to class already familiar with the material you otherwise would have presented in a lecture.

You then decide to transform the challenging environment that an auditorium poses to your active learning strategies into an asset. On some days, you have students work with a partner either behind them or in the next row as part of the **think-pair-share** technique discussed in this chapter. On other days, you break the class into six smaller groups—one at each corner of the room, and two in different sections of the seating area—to devise questions for the other groups that you use as part of a **game-based learning** strategy. Once the questions have been developed, the auditorium provides the perfect environment for a "game show experience" in which the different groups compete with one another.

EFFECTIVE TEACHING IN OTHER SETTINGS

Of course, not every course a college professor teaches enrolls a large number of students. Even though class sizes are increasing at many institutions, there are still many opportunities to teach smaller sections, seminars, and courses that meet in traditional classrooms as well as other academic settings, such as laboratories, studios, libraries, and online environments. These courses offer college professors abundant opportunities to get away from the "teaching is telling" model and to engage students in activities where their learning becomes much more active and effective. Among the most common techniques used to increase the level of active learning in small classes are the following:

- The **Socratic Method** is a strategy by which teachers don't tell students the answer to a question but allow them to discover possible answers on their own by guiding them through a series of questions. This technique is equally useful regardless of whether the questions posed by the professor have a single correct answer, no correct answer, or several potentially correct answers depending on the situation. Named for the ancient Greek philosopher Socrates (469–399 BCE), who used it to help students realize that they didn't understand certain concepts as well as they thought they did, the Socratic method is particularly useful in getting people to challenge their own assumptions, defend a line of reasoning, and think on their feet.
- **Case Studies**, which were mentioned briefly earlier, are real or hypothetical situations that pose a problem that students are expected to solve. In law and business schools, for instance, case studies are descriptions of actual events that illustrate a particular legal principle or a challenge in such areas as marketing, management, product design, business ethics, and so on. In philosophy and education courses, case studies may be based on actual events but are frequently fictionalized so as to make them more complex and challenging as *thought experiments*. One particular strength of the case studies approach is that it allows students to understand immediately the relationship between theory and practice and to relate course content to real-world experiences. That's one of the reasons why the authors have

incorporated so many hypothetical case studies and scenarios into this book.

- **Experiential Learning** is a term applied to any situation in which students learn by doing rather than by listening or observing. While laboratory courses are perhaps the most familiar type of experiential learning, this approach can be used in nearly every discipline. For example, simulations are used to train pilots, nuclear power plant operators, financial planners, and physicians in a way that allows them to develop their skills before they are actually placed in a situation that could jeopardize the health or well-being of others. Community service learning provides students with experience in applying the techniques they learn in their coursework to real-life situations by benefiting the public. In other courses, experiential learning can be introduced through the **Explain-Demonstrate-Do** technique in which a procedure is first explained by the instructor (an approach that appeals to students who prefer to learn through oral instruction), then demonstrated by the instructor (which appeals to visual learners), and finally is performed by the students themselves (which appeals to experiential learners).

- **Critiques** are a particular form of experiential learning in which a student is coached by an instructor as a way of the student's performance. Studio art courses, music instruction, and physical education classes are common examples of how critiques may be used in college courses: The student engages in an activity that he or she has been practicing, receives constructive criticism on how to improve, and seeks to incorporate that criticism into an improved performance. But this strategy works well for other disciplines as well. In a course on counseling, for instance, the instructor could critique a student's performance during a simulation or case study and then determine whether the outcome is better when the student applies the advice he or she received. Critiques of software coding can be used to help students design routines that are more concise and professional. Critiques of the bedside manner of students pursuing one of the health professions can help them become more compassionate and effective. Critiques of the oral or written performance of students in any course can help improve their communication skills.

CASE STUDY 1.3:
THE NON-COMMUNICATIVE STUDENT

You are teaching a graduate seminar in your discipline to a group of twelve master's degree students. Most of them are doing quite well. They arrive for class well prepared, introduce valid perspectives into the discussion, and seem to be enjoying the material tremendously. Only one student is causing you great concern. Wally Blank, a second-year graduate student, contributes almost nothing to class discussions and, even when asked direct questions, tends to answer only in monosyllables. This is the first of your courses in which Wally has enrolled, so you don't know much about his history and past performance.

When you examine Wally's transcript, you discover that his performance has been satisfactory, though not stellar, with most grades being either A minus or B. Baffled about what to do next, you invite Wally to meet with you in an informal conference. You explain that you're concerned about his lack of participation in class, emphasize how important active student involvement is to the course's success, and ask whether there's anything Wally can share about why he's been so unresponsive in class. The conversation seems to go nowhere. Wally provides little eye contact, answers each question with only a few words, and provides no greater insight than that "everything is fine."

Wally's advisor is one of your friends in the department, and so you feel free to ask whether there's anything else you need to know that might help Wally succeed. The response you receive isn't very helpful. "Oh, Wally Blank? Yes, he's a weird one all right. Always does his homework but never says anything at all in class unless you press him. He's the same when I have my advising appointments with him. He can't really tell me why he's in this field or what his long-range plans are. I'm not sure he knows. He probably won't complete the degree. If I were you, I wouldn't worry about it. You can't save them all, you know. Our job is simply to educate the students. We can't motivate them, too. The motivation has to come from them. If they don't have that degree of motivation within them, there's nothing we can do to provide it."

Questions

1. What do you do?
   a. Is your colleague correct? Is it up to Wally to succeed or fail on his own and not your job to motivate what appears to be a disengaged student?
   b. Is your colleague's suggestion ill-advised? Is there any way in which it *is* the role of a college professor to motivate students, even if they are at the graduate level and already strongly committed to the discipline?
   c. Is there any way in which your handling of the situation so far may have increased Wally's reserve and lack of willingness to participate in class?
2. Would your response be different if one of the following were true?
   a. If there were strong suspicion among the rest of the faculty that Wally Blank may have a condition that falls somewhere on the Asperger/autism spectrum. When you make an inquiry to the Office of Student Disabilities, however, you're told, "We don't have any request for accommodation on file from Wally Blank. And I'm afraid that I'm not at liberty to share any other information with you."
   b. If Wally were a veteran who returned from several consecutive tours of combat duty less than six months before beginning your program.
   c. If Wally were involved in an automobile accident several years ago that was determined to be his fault and in which several people died, including his own sister.
   d. If, except for your friend who is Wally's advisor, none of the other faculty members in the program had had a similar experience with Wally. In fact, one colleague says, "Wally Blank? Oh, he did fine in my two courses last year. Got an A from me each term. His oral and written work was all quite good."

Resolution

You decide that, even though your friend may be correct that "you can't save them all," you're not quite ready to give up on Wally Blank. If

Wally was good enough to be admitted to your graduate program, you owe him every effort you can possibly make to help him succeed.

As a result, you decide to vary your teaching strategies to see if you can find a format best suited to Wally's individual needs. For one assignment, you have each student prepare a one-page reaction paper to a case study described in the textbook and read that reaction paper aloud during the next class session. Each student is then required to respond to each other student's reaction paper in a single sentence. Although you say that your reason for restricting comments in this way is to allow everyone a chance to speak and to compel each student to be as concise as possible, you're actually trying to level the playing field for Wally so that everyone in the class has to speak for just as long as he does.

You also become quite inventive in trying to find other ways for students to participate in class. For example, one day you challenge each student to bring in a single graphic that best represents a key concept covered by that day's assignment. On another occasion, you cancel the class meeting since you happen to be away at a conference but have the students participate in an online chat about the course material through your institution's course management system. For a third class, you have the students once again prepare reaction papers. But, instead of reading them aloud in class, they spend the session reading and preparing anonymous written critiques of each other's work.

None of these strategies provides a sudden breakthrough by improving Wally's class participation dramatically. Nevertheless, by the end of the term, you conclude that Wally's class participation has improved sufficiently to earn an A minus from you. You hope that you can continue to build on this progress in successive courses, and so you encourage Wally to enroll in another one of your classes next term.

FOR REFLECTION

As college professors, we often turn to our colleagues for advice, support, and understanding. In the authors' survey of faculty members, they asked participants for the best advice on teaching they could give other professors, particularly those who are just starting out. Here's a sample of what those taking the survey recommended.

- Keep a sense of humor and remember that students really do want to learn.
- For every course you teach, seek out and provide personal help for at least one student who is struggling.
- Get to know your students as individuals. Make your teaching personal.
- Find a mentor in your field and work closely with that person as you develop your own philosophy of teaching.
- Be flexible, creative, and patient.
- Model the engagement you expect of your students. If you want to foster discussion, start getting students to talk during the very first class. If you want them to come to class prepared, make sure that you're always prepared for every single class you teach.
- Try not to replicate your graduate school experience in the undergraduate classroom. Undergraduates have very different outlooks and approaches to the material you're teaching. Work to understand them on their own terms.

2

PROMOTING STUDENT
SUCCESS AND ENGAGEMENT

The term *student success* is often used to encompass a large number of related goals.

- High student retention from term to term
- Reduction of the number of students who receive low grades or withdraw from courses, particularly when those courses are required
- The development of each student as a "whole person" as demonstrated by a high level of student engagement with both coursework and cocurricular activities
- The ability of each student to identify a specific career plan and/or set of life goals
- Timely progress made by each student toward graduation
- Placement after graduation in a career closely related to the student's field, a program of further education, or some other opportunity that reflects the student's life goals

Certainly the most important contribution a college professor can make toward promoting student success is to create the type of active, rich learning environments that we explored in the previous chapter.

But our role in student success isn't limited to the courses we teach. It has long been recognized that the single greatest factor contributing to student retention and timely progress toward graduation is the *relationship students have with individual faculty members*. (See, for example, Chickering & Gamson, 1987; Habley, Bloom, & Robbins, 2012, 34; Coburn & Treeger, 2009, 268–70; and Kuh, Schuh, & Whitt, 1991). Students who become actively involved with a campus band, chorus, play, athletic team, honors program, or club often do better than students who are less involved in activities precisely because these activities enable them to develop close relationships with faculty members that extend beyond the classroom. We call this effect the *concierge principle of student success:* Just as the concierge of a hotel makes guests feel pampered and special by tending to their needs, so does close student-faculty interaction help students feel appreciated as individuals, understood, valued, and accepted. Students are also less likely to want to let down a professor to whom they feel close by performing poorly in a course or failing to graduate, and so they redouble their efforts to make sure they live up to the professor's expectations. After all, it's one thing to receive a D from "my organic chemistry teacher"; it's another thing entirely not to have tried your hardest for "Professor Jones."

In some cases, the relationship that students develop with faculty members can last an entire lifetime. As part of a survey that the authors sent to hundreds of college professors, faculty members were asked how often they heard from former students after they graduated. (The phrase *heard from* was defined as including personal visits, phone calls, emails, letters, and other substantive contact. Respondents were urged not to include updates posted to Facebook, Twitter, Instagram, and other social media sites unless the student's messages were addressed to them personally rather than to the general public. Respondents were also asked not to include requests for letters of recommendation and other favors that the faculty members were being asked to perform on behalf of the students who contacted them.) By far the most common answers were once or twice a year (41.1 percent of respondents chose this option) and several times each academic term (35.2 percent). Far smaller groups of faculty members said that former students tended to contact them several times a month (11.7 percent) or less often than once or twice a year (5.5 percent). Only a negligible number of respondents said they were contacted by former students more than several times a week, and not a single respondent reported that he or she had never been contacted by a former student at all.

The conclusion to draw from these results is that the impact individual college professors make on students is greater than we sometimes believe. During a particularly difficult year, it can be tempting to conclude that no one is interested in the material we are teaching, the students are simply taking our courses in order to receive a diploma, and what we do as professors makes very little difference in the grand scheme of things. But the survey conducted by the authors suggests something quite different. *Every* college professor makes a difference in *someone*'s life. While not all students will care enough to contact an instructor years later, a sufficient number of them go through the trouble to find out where we are now and how to get in touch with us, so we receive updates from students we taught even several decades earlier. This, then, is one of the great challenges of work as a college professor: We're shaping lives in ways that we often don't see for many years. We don't witness students having those "Aha!" moments as often as we might like. But those moments do occur, and it is how we relate to students that helps bring them about.

One of the reasons why our relationship with students is so important is that our students tend to see us as mentors and seek our advice on a broad range of issues. In the authors' survey, college professors were asked how often their current students discussed with them personal matters that had little or nothing to do with the courses they were teaching. These conversations, according to 5.8 percent of the respondents, occurred several times a week! Another 23.5 percent reported that such conversations occurred several times a month, while 35.2 percent (the largest group) said these conversations took place several times each academic term. Less than one-third, 29.4 percent of respondents mentioned they only have this type of conversation with students once or twice a year. Only 6.1 percent of the professors answering the survey said that students talked to them about personal matters more rarely than once or twice a year. So, even if you've never viewed yourself as a counselor or mentor, for college professors, that type of consultation simply goes with the job.

CASE STUDY 2.1: HOW CLOSE IS TOO CLOSE?

One day you receive a call from Dr. Novice, a faculty member at your institution who's currently in his second year. "I've got a problem," Dr. Novice tells you nervously, "and I need your advice." Over the next several minutes he outlines for you a situation that's been unfolding over the last week.

As part of your school's orientation program for new faculty, a great deal of attention is always given to the importance of building close relationships between students and faculty members. Doctor Novice attended these workshops and has been making himself available several hours each week at a local coffee shop to meet with any of his students who want to stop by and talk. While attendance at these events has been mixed—at times only a single student shows up, even when many more said they would be there—Dr. Novice has concluded that the events are successful enough to continue.

A little more than a week ago, Dr. Novice decided to carry this experiment a bit further. He invited the members of his junior seminar to his house for dinner. The seminar only enrolls eighteen students and, although Dr. Novice's home is small, he was sure that he could accommodate that many guests. Sixteen of his students said that they were free on the night of the dinner and would attend.

When his classes were over on the day of the dinner, Dr. Novice spent several hours cooking and getting the house ready for his students. The first student to arrive, Kaley Reticent, had often joined Dr. Novice for coffee. In fact, she was the one student who would attend these informal sessions even if no other students bothered to show up. Kaley is a very quiet, introverted student, but Dr. Novice made the best of the situation, keeping the conversation going and hoping that another student would arrive soon.

Forty-five minutes after the scheduled time of the dinner had passed, and no one else from the class had yet appeared. Dr. Novice briefly considered canceling the dinner and taking Kaley back to campus for a meal in the dining hall, but rejected this idea because he had already prepared so much food. He decided that he and Kaley would eat the dinner he'd made, and then he'd cut the evening short and allow Kaley to return to her residence hall.

Once the meal was over, however, and Dr. Novice escorted Kaley to the door, he realized at once why none of the other students had arrived and why he now had a problem to deal with: a late season snowstorm had left drifts nearly three feet high before his front door and rendered the roads completely blocked. Before he could think of how to respond, he heard Kaley say, "It looks like I'm not going anywhere now. Guess I'll have to stay the night."

Questions

1. Based only on what you know so far, what do you believe Dr. Novice should have done at this point?

2. It's obvious that Dr. Novice was worried about how people might interpret his dinner alone with a student who then spends the night at his house.

    a. To what extent was the problem Dr. Novice's fault in that he could have taken steps to avoid such an uncomfortable situation from occurring? In other words, should this situation have been foreseeable?

    b. To what extent was the problem simply a chain of unfortunate events that Dr. Novice could not have foreseen and now had to make the best of?

3. Dr. Novice has called you for advice. What advice would you give if he concluded his story in one of the following ways?

    a. "I made up the guest bedroom and had Kaley return to campus as soon as roads were clear in the morning. Now all I can think about is what people are going to assume if this story ever gets out."

    b. "She then told me how much she liked me, became very flirtatious, and said she was glad we'd have so much time together. I told her that I was sorry if I had given her the wrong impression, saw myself only as her professor, and didn't want there to be any misunderstanding between us. She got angry and left the first thing in the morning. Now she's claiming that I led her on and is threatening to file a sexual harassment complaint against me."

    c. "We had a good laugh at how ridiculous the situation was. She slept on my couch and was gone before I even woke up in the morning. But now she's telling other students that I'm her boyfriend and letting them assume that more happened that night than really occurred."

    d. "She's so quiet that our conversation was very strained for the rest of the evening. I decided that the best thing to do was for us to watch movies in my living room. By 4:00 a.m., we both must have fallen asleep in our chairs. She left as soon as she could the next morning. But now she hasn't been to class since that evening and, when I was about to pass her walking across campus, she ducked into a building to avoid me. I think she's embarrassed."

4. Would your advice be any different if Dr. Novice were a woman
   and the student involved were male? Would it change if both of
   them were the same gender?

Resolution

You begin by telling Dr. Novice that there's a clear line between
our being highly accessible to students and crossing the boundaries of
our professional relationships. The goal, you continue, should be to be
"friendly, not familiar" so that there's no possibility that our relationship
with students will be misinterpreted by anyone, including the students
themselves. You say, "Since Kaley was the only student who showed up
sometimes at your informal discussions over coffee, you should have foreseen the possibility that she'd be the only one to come to your dinner."

You go on to stress the importance of avoiding situations that can lead
to this kind of predicament. "It may be unfair," you go on, "to say that
it's okay for married professors to have students over to their house for
dinner when they're sure their spouse will be around, while it's not ad-
visable for a single faculty member to do the same, but that's the world
we live in. People will often assume the worst, and even students might
misinterpret our intentions if we aren't careful. At the very least, you
should have called your department chair when you realized that you
were snowed in, worked out a plan together, and thus kept your supervisor informed as to what was happening."

Since you can't change the past, however, you next try to focus on what
you should recommend as the situation moves forward. You advise Dr.
Novice to inform his chair immediately and also to call the office that deals
with sexual harassment issues (at most institutions the proper place would
be the office of equal opportunity programs or the campus ombudsman).
You say, "I don't mean to frighten you, but you might also want to touch
base with your own lawyer, just to get legal advice on how to proceed."

One complicating factor in this case is Kaley Reticent's quiet and
reserved nature. It may be difficult to determine how she's feeling and
what her concerns are. After Dr. Novice discusses the matter with his
chair, a decision is made to schedule an informal conversation with
Kaley, her advisor, and a representative from the office of student affairs. The goal is to achieve a balance between making more of the situation than it is and ignoring the student's needs and desires.

Dr. Novice would be told that a number of outcomes could follow from that discussion: The case may be considered resolved, with the understanding that he'll avoid uncomfortable situations like this one in the future; Kaley may be transferred from his section to one taught by a different professor; if Kaley does file a sexual harassment complaint, that process will play out and steps will be taken to protect both her rights and his; or some other appropriate resolution will be implemented.

PROMOTING STUDENT SUCCESS THROUGH ENGAGEMENT

In *How People Learn* (2003), John Bransford, Ann Brown, Suzanne Donovan, and James Pellegrino review the evidence provided by numerous studies in neuroscience, cognitive psychology, and epistemology to identify the most effective practices we can engage in as college professors in order to promote student success. Several of the practices they recommend are relatively easy to implement.

The first of these practices is *metacognition* (sometimes also known as *metathinking*), the conscious awareness of one's own process of learning, solving problems, and recognizing patterns among seemingly unrelated bits of information. Metacognition is responsible for a phenomenon familiar to every college professor: We knew our fields well when we were students, but we only really mastered them when we had to teach these subjects to others. When we explain a concept to someone else, we have to look at it differently and, in so doing, we become aware not only of what we know, but also of *how we know it*.

We can encourage our students to begin developing that advanced level of mastery by having them give us, not merely correct answers to test questions, but a summary of how they knew those answers were correct. Math teachers have been doing this for years. That's why every math test we can remember included the instruction "Show your work." But we're often less likely to make similar requests of students in history, business, literature, marketing, educational leadership, philosophy, psychology, human relations, and other classes. And yet, if we omit this important step, we're depriving ourselves of one of the best tools in our toolkits for helping students succeed.

The use of **metacognition** can be as simple as asking students, not to solve a problem or answer a question but to describe the process they'd use *in order to* solve the problem or answer the question. While that approach certainly has many possibilities for classroom activities and exam questions, it is also useful for interactions with students when they come to us as their advisors and mentors. For example, when we explore careers and other life choices with them, we may be doing a greater service by guiding them through the *process* of making a decision rather than by offering them *alternative choices* for that decision.

The second practice by which we can help increase student success is **intentionality**. People tend to learn better when they develop clear plans for their learning, even though those plans will inevitably change—and sometimes be entirely replaced—as their learning continues. Like metacognition, intentionality can occur on many different levels. At the micro level, as students read their textbooks and complete their assignments, they can:

- **preview the activity:** What do they expect to learn from the chapter they are about to read or the activity they are going to perform?
- **anticipate questions:** What do they believe may challenge them or prove to be difficult in the new material?
- **compare expectations with reality:** When they completed the assignment, did they learn what they expected? What was easier or harder than they thought it would be? What still remains unclear?

At the macro level, students can begin to think about the difference they would like to make in the world. In the movie, *Dead Poets Society* (1989), an instructor named Mr. Keating (played by Robin Williams) challenges his students to make their lives extraordinary. What would our own students do in order to make their lives extraordinary?

The third recommended practice is **mindfulness**, awareness of the activities we are performing while we are performing them. So often we do things on autopilot. We get to the end of a meal unable to recall what it was we just ate or arrive at work in the morning unable to describe a single thing we saw along the way. Students, too, are often on autopilot while they're studying. They may characterize what they're doing as *multitasking*, but what is actually occurring is that their attention is on the music they're listening to or the texts they're receiving rather than the book they're supposedly reading. Mindfulness on the micro level can consist of asking themselves at the end of each paragraph they read, "What was the most important thing I just read? How can I paraphrase it in my own words?" On a larger scale, mindfulness could consist of pondering what students are doing today (or at least this semester) in order to achieve their goal of making their lives extraordinary.

The fourth practice is **reflection**, which is in some ways the counter-balance to intentionality. For each activity that they engage in as part of their development, what has worked well? What would they have done differently? What general patterns can they see that can help them continue their learning and development in the future? How would they explain these insights to others? How do their new insights relate to what they already knew? This last question is particularly important since people learn best when they can see some connection between new insights and prior knowledge. Drawing those connections is an important step in integrating new learning into their existing understanding and making new information their own.

The fifth and final practice that we'll consider in this chapter is **immersion**. If you've ever known a student who made very little progress in learning a language despite several semesters of study, but who seemed to become almost fluent after spending a summer abroad, you've seen the power of immersion at work. Colleges and universities sometimes try to immerse their students in an academic environment by creating *living-learning communities*, residential arrangements in which students take several courses together while living in proximity to one another in a residence hall. At times, these living-learning communities have disciplinary themes (a French house, leadership wing, pre-med floor, and the like), while others simply group students who are at similar points in their academic programs. The goal is to extend learning beyond the classroom and to extend social development into the class-room: Participants are more likely to form study groups and to discuss academic issues outside of class when they live near students who share their academic experiences; they're more likely to form bonds with people in their residence halls if they also attend classes with them.

That type of complete academic immersion isn't possible for every course a student takes. But college professors can gain some of the benefits of an immersion experience by creating a virtual community of their students through a course management system. In the survey of faculty members conducted by the authors, participants were asked what percentage of their courses included an online course management system like Blackboard, Moodle, or Edmodo as a substantive component of how they taught. In other words, how often did they use this type of software not simply to calculate and post grades, send email, distribute course readings, and conduct other peripheral course functions but to continue the learning experience of the students beyond the classroom. The responses fell into three roughly equivalent groups. About a third of the college professors said they used a course management system in every course they taught. Almost the same number said they never used such a system. And approximately a third fell somewhere in the middle. The latter group could be broken into four subgroups, all of about the same size.

1. Those who answered, "Perhaps not every single course, but around two-thirds or three-quarters of the courses I teach." (This answer was favored slightly more than the next three choices, but not significantly.)
2. Those who use course management systems extensively in approximately half of the courses they teach.
3. Those who use this type of software in fewer than half of the courses they teach.
4. Those who use it in only a handful of the courses they teach.

CASE STUDY 2.2: MAKING THE STUDENT EXPERIENCE MORE ENGAGING

Imagine that you are asked to serve as a mentor to several faculty members who want to increase their students' level of success. Each of them shows you an assignment or exam question that he or she has used in the past. Use one or more of the following strategies to recommend a way in which that exercise could be improved:

- metacognition
- intentionality
- mindfulness
- reflection
- immersion

The first professor teaches world history and traditionally has students write a short analysis paper on the following question: "Many different dates and reasons have been assigned to the fall of the ancient Roman empire. Choose one of these dates and argue why you believe it is the most accurate. Be sure also to identify the *reasons* why you believe Rome fell at this time."

The second professor teaches sociology and has often included the following question on exams in the introductory course: "Identify the original four stages of group development as proposed by Bruce Tuckman. How did Tuckman later revise this model with Mary Ann Jensen to include a fifth stage?"

A chemistry professor is in the group you're mentoring and frequently asks students the following question on a pop quiz: "What types of material are most likely to be affected by acid rain? How could someone diminish the likelihood of damage to this material if it could not be moved indoors or protected by any type of shelter?"

The fourth professor teaches finite mathematics and frequently includes some version of the following question as a homework assignment: "How many different combinations of four numbers can be made within a set of sixteen numbers? How many permutations of four numbers can be made? Which of these two numbers is larger? Why?"

The fifth professor you're mentoring teaches marketing and often includes the following question on the final exam of introductory courses: "What are the four phases of the typical product life cycle? Which of these phases is typically the most challenging for businesses? What are appropriate actions for businesses to take during this phase?"

Questions

1. Would your advice to the faculty members be any different if the students in the course consisted wholly of one of the following?
   a. majors in that discipline
   b. non-majors in that discipline
   c. transfer students from abroad whose life experience is distinctly different from that of most North American students
2. Would your advice to the faculty members be any different if the platform for course delivery were one of the following?
   a. completely online

   b. completely in-person
   c. a hybrid of online and in-person platforms
3. Would your advice to the faculty members be any different if the
   people you were mentoring consisted solely of one of the following?
   a. untenured junior faculty members who only recently received
      their doctorates
   b. mid-career faculty members who are working toward promo-
      tion to the rank of full professor
   c. senior faculty members who were criticized for the quality of
      their instruction in a post-tenure review process and assigned
      to you for remediation

Resolution

One pattern you see repeated throughout these assignments and
questions is that they largely deal with concepts in the abstract rather
than tying them to specific examples. For this reason, some students
will have difficulty relating these ideas to their prior learning and understanding how to apply them to new situations as they arise.

Another pattern you will recognize is that some of the questions rely
heavily on memorization. If a student, for whatever reason, can't recall
the possible dates for the fall of Rome that were discussed in class or the
textbook, Tuckman's four stages of group development, or the four phases
of a product's life cycle, he or she can't then proceed to any higher order
analysis, synthesis, application, or evaluation of these principles.

You begin, therefore, by challenging the five professors to think of
more creative ways to achieve their desired outcomes while helping
the students succeed by relating the concepts to their own experience
or prior knowledge. You ask them to think of ways of evaluating the
students' mastery of these concepts that doesn't necessarily include
traditional homework assignments, quizzes, or exams. After a week, the
professors return to you with their ideas.

The history professor decides to use the **co-teaching** and **jigsaw
group** techniques that we explored in the last chapter in a revised
exercise on the fall of Rome. Each student is assigned to two groups:
one will specialize in one of the possible dates for this event (such as
Diocletian's division of the empire into four prefectures in 293 CE, the

abdication of Romulus Augustulus in 476 CE, and Justinian's closing of the philosophical schools occurred in 529 CE) and the other of which will specialize in causal factors (such as technological stagnation, the failure to develop a consistent system for imperial succession, the influx of nomadic tribes into Roman territories, and the rise of new religions). When the students break into their date-based groups, the job of each student is to explain to the others how the causal factor in which he or she specializes plays a role in that period. When the students break into their causal factor groups, their job is to explain the degree to which that factor was important at the date in which they specialize.

The sociology professor will bring poster boards labeled with each of the phases of group development in the Tuckman/Jensen model: forming, norming, storming, and adjourning or mourning. The class will then be broken into five subgroups, each of which will gather by one of the poster boards. For ten minutes, they are to discuss how that stage of group development was illustrated by a group to which they have belonged, such as a sports team, club, or school group. After ten minutes, they will rotate to the next poster board in a clockwise direction and continue the exercise. In this way, each student can relate the theory to his or her own experience within a single fifty-minute class.

The chemistry professor decides to retain the issue of acid rain as a pop quiz topic but will make it easier for the students to relate to. Instead of being asked about the concept in a general way, they'll be given the following scenario: "Imagine that you're hired as a consultant to a city where the façades of each building are made of the following substances (only one substance per building): marble, limestone, concrete, glass interspersed with nickel-chromium steel, and aluminum alloy. Because of the size of the buildings it is impossible to shelter their exteriors completely. Your job is to set a priority order for which buildings are most at risk for damage from acid rain and to develop a workable strategy for protecting those surfaces."

The math professor similarly decides to retain the question about combinations and permutations as a homework assignment but phrases it in a manner to which the students can relate more readily: "Imagine that you are in a class of sixteen students. How many different study groups of four students each can be formed from those sixteen students? After the first test, the students will be ranked from first to fourth according to their scores: How many of these four-ranked-student possible outcomes could be developed for the whole class?"

The marketing professor rewrites the final exam question as follows: "Imagine that you're the CEO of a company that has been marketing the same product for twenty years. Although sales grew during the first fifteen years the product was available, they have steadily declined for the past five years. What options are available to you in addressing this issue?"

In order to include elements of metacognition, the students will be asked in each case not only to provide an answer but also to summarize the process they used to arrive at that answer. In order to include elements of intentionality and reflection, they will be asked first to provide an educated guess as to what they believe each answer would be, next go through a systematic process of answering the question, and finally compare the answer they obtained to their original estimate and explain any differences between them.

ADDRESSING PROBLEMS WITH STUDENTS

While in the best of all possible worlds, every interaction we have with students would be pleasant, every student would be dedicated to his or her studies and committed to high levels of academic achievement, and every course we teach would be filled with well prepared, highly motivated students, this utopian scenario doesn't reflect the real world. Problems with students can range from minor annoyances to major issues that threaten our job satisfaction and even our safety. In their survey of college professors, the authors found that nearly a quarter of respondents, 23.5 percent, noted they felt their safety had been in danger at least once in their careers because of what a student had said or done.

Somewhat surprisingly it turned out that those answers had absolutely no correlation with how long the faculty member had been teaching. In other words, it wasn't the case that more experienced faculty members were more likely to report that they'd once felt threatened by a student simply because they had been in the profession longer. Ominous situations can occur regardless of a college professor's age, gender, and experience. For this reason, one of the components colleges and universities ought to consider including in their faculty development programs is how people should handle situations where they believe they are no longer safe because of a student's words or actions.

Turning to less severe types of challenges, the authors then asked college professors how annoyed they were when students texted or used their electronic devices for non-course-related purposes in class. They responded as follows:

- 44.4 percent said they were extremely annoyed.
- 38.8 percent reported being quite annoyed.
- 11.1 percent were not very annoyed.
- 5.5 percent were not at all annoyed.

With more than 83 percent of those who were surveyed expressing at least some degree of frustration at the use of electronic devices in class, it's clear that keeping students engaged in the course material can often be a challenge. Since increasing numbers of students are using laptop computers, tablets, and smartphones for note-taking and as replacements for traditional textbooks, it's important for faculty members to explore ways of making these devices an integral part of the learning process, rather than a mere distraction.

One method for achieving this goal is to take advantage of electronic survey sites, such as polleverywhere.com, to provide frequent mini-quizzes, opinion polls, attitude checks, and in-class exercises. This strategy shifts the use of the electronic device from recreational to pedagogical purposes, can provide an instant snapshot of which students are attending (and paying attention in) class, and offers feedback on whether the class is mastering the material at the rate the instructor expects. Many course management systems also offer tablet and smartphone apps that college professors can use to keep students engaged during class. Websites like everyslide.com allow students to follow along with PowerPoint or Keynote presentations in class and provide interactive maps and polls with results that can be immediately incorporated into the professor's presentation.

ASSISTANCE AND REMEDIATION FOR STUDENT SUCCESS

Just as in the best of all possible worlds every encounter with a student would be pleasant, so would we want every student in our classes to be capable of performing college-level work successfully and independently.

Unfortunately, this second utopian vision is also very different from the reality most college professors face. Students sometimes reach us unprepared for work at the level they need to succeed in their courses and without the tools they need in order to remediate these deficiencies themselves.

The fact of the matter is that some students don't know how to use certain higher-order thinking skills like analysis, synthesis, creativity, and innovative application *because these skills weren't necessary to succeed in high school*. As a result, some students find that engaging in the same activities that got them As in their earlier schooling now may not even earn them passing grades. They may feel that *studying* is the same thing as *learning* even though the time they put in memorizing terms and solving sample problem sets doesn't prepare them to recognize patterns in a diverse set of data, apply concepts to new situations, or develop new ways of addressing problems no one has encountered before.

SCENARIO 2.1

Imagine that you've imposed a strict classroom policy that students may not use electronic devices in class because you want their full attention to be directed to the course material. Before class one day, a student brings you a letter from the office of students with disabilities validating that the student has a learning disability and must be offered the accommodation of taking notes on an electronic tablet or smartphone. You agree that this accommodation constitutes an exception to your policy and allow the student to take notes by means of an electronic device.

Challenge Question:

Without violating the student's rights to privacy (as specified by HIPAA—the Health Insurance Portability and Accountability Act of 1996—and your institution's own policies), how do you respond to questions from students who say to you, "I thought you never allowed the use of electronic devices in class. Why can that one student use a cell phone or tablet in class when I can't?"

Scenario Outcome:

You tell anyone who asks that you respect each person's right to privacy and thus won't go into any specific details of any individual student's situation. Nevertheless, you express your belief that even the most stringent policy can have an exception if there's a sufficiently compelling reason. You express your willingness to let this student also take notes on an electronic device—if the student will bring you written documentation from a qualified professional that taking notes in this way is essential to his or her academic success.

SCENARIO 2.2

Following the scenario just outlined, you are distracted several times in class one day by some whispering and giggling that is occurring near the back of the room. You let it go the first few times but then decide to stroll around the room to see what's happening. You observe that the student who was granted the accommodation to use an electronic device in class has been using it to access social media and other websites that have nothing to do with the course material. The students sitting nearby are the ones whose whispering and giggling you've heard.

Challenge Question:

How do you deal with this situation?

Scenario Outcome:

You remind the student with the electronic device to pay attention during class. As the students are leaving the room at the end of class, you ask the student to speak with you for a moment. "When I agreed to let you use your tablet or smartphone in class," you say in a part of the room where the other students won't overhear the conversation, "it was because of the accommodation specified by the office of students with disabilities. That accommodation was for you to take notes, not update your Facebook status or browse websites. In the future, if there are incidents like what happened today, I'll have to speak to the director of the office of students with disabilities to see what other options we might have."

SCENARIO 2.3

Several days after resolving the situation described in the previous scenario, you're teaching the same class when you notice that a different student is frequently looking at a cell phone, grimacing, and setting the phone aside, only to pick it up again a short time later. Since this behavior is distracting you (even if no one else appears to notice it), you finally say. "I'd just like to remind everyone of my policy that electronic devices can't be used in this class unless you've received my prior authorization to do so for valid reasons. Please put your devices away and refrain from taking them out again until the class is over."

The response surprises you. The student in question stands up and begins to argue with you. "Hey! Don't humiliate me by singling me out like that! I may not have as many degrees as you, but I deserve your respect!" You tell the student to sit down and say that you were stating a general policy, not singling anyone out. Rather than resolving the situation, however, your remark merely seems to fan the flames. The student becomes more and more belligerent, loud, and less coherent. Students who were sitting nearby begin to move away. Eventually, the student begins to step between the other seats and move toward you.

Challenge Question:

How do you respond?

Scenario Outcome:

There's a clear distinction between rude behavior and aggressive actions that threaten the safety of others. This student has now crossed that line. Your first concern must be for the safety of the other students and yourself. You use your cell phone to call campus security (or 911), dismiss the class, and begin to clear the room. Help arrives even before all the students have had a chance to leave. You briefly explain why you called, and the officers take the student into custody. The matter may be one for the police to deal with, or it may best be addressed within the student judicial system at your institution. But that can be decided later. Your first concern had to be for the safety of everyone concerned, and the wisest decision was not to take any chances.

In addition to the five practices for promoting student engagement mentioned earlier, college professors need other tools in their toolkits to provide assistance and remediation to students who need one or both in order to succeed. One of these tools is assisting students in breaking down what may seem to them to be a single, vague concept (studying) into a series of systematic actions that can lead to mastery of the material in their courses (learning). For example students can be encouraged to engage in the following success strategies for every class period on their schedules:

1. *Look backward to look forward*: Students should ask themselves such questions as "What were the most important ideas covered in our last class and in our assignment for today?" and "How do I expect these concepts will relate to today's topic as indicated on the course syllabus?"

2. *Be fully present*: Students can't learn if they don't attend class. But they also can't learn unless they're fully engaged in every class. Encourage them to take notes beyond what the professor writes on the board or includes in a PowerPoint presentation. Tell them that, at each moment they're in class, they should be able to answer the question, "What is the concept the professor is currently covering?" Remind them that it's not uncommon for there to be more than one important concept in a single class meeting.

3. *Review immediately*: Students shouldn't wait until the next test to review their notes. Instead they should read over them and try to paraphrase them as soon as possible after a class is over. One good way of doing so is to take notes on paper while in class and then rewrite them in a word processing file soon after class. This practice has an added advantage in that, if the paper notes are lost, there will still be a backup copy.

4. *Study effectively*: Students do better when they review material in several short sessions than in a single long session of cramming. Encourage them to review class notes and textbook material (as well as do additional sample problems in courses where that is possible) for at least an hour twice a week, even when no exam is scheduled.

5. *Explain material to others*: Sometimes our thoughts don't really become clear until we try to explain a concept to others. (As we saw

earlier, many of us who are college professors found that we never thoroughly understood certain ideas until we had to teach them to others.) Study groups, working with a friend or family member, and even summarizing material aloud when no one else is around can be beneficial ways of understanding material more systematically.

6. *Use your resources*: For ideas that simply don't become clear despite the earlier steps, encourage students to meet with the professor or teaching assistant during office hours. Ask them to come with specific questions instead of saying something general like, "I just don't get this." At the very least, they should try to specify at which point in a process their understanding breaks down. For more complex challenges, the office of students with disabilities can also be a helpful resource. There students can be tested to see if they have a recognized learning disability or another type of challenge they weren't aware of earlier.

CASE STUDY 2.3: WHAT IS THE PROFESSOR'S OBLIGATION?

You're teaching an intermediate class of about forty students who are majoring in your discipline. Most of the students are doing fairly well, but one appears to be struggling terribly. Homework assignments are turned in with some questions left entirely unanswered, others with just a series of question marks scrawled in the margin, and still others with answers that are wrong but you can tell what the student was thinking that led to the error. On one test, the student's sole answer to a question that was intended to produce a multi-paragraph essay was, "What's the point?"

You can't quite tell whether the student is lost or bored in class. In any case, you rarely if ever see the student taking notes, and you've never known the student to volunteer an answer or opinion during a discussion. In fact, the only time you've ever heard the student speak is once when you asked a direct question. On that occasion, you were somewhat surprised to hear the student provide an answer that seemed well considered and properly argued. You fear that this student won't succeed in the major unless there's a significant improvement in performance on assignments, quizzes, and tests.

Questions

1. Where does your responsibility to help this student succeed end and his or her own responsibility for good performance begin?
2. Are there circumstances in which you would feel that the best approach is to do nothing and let the student figure out how to succeed independently?
3. If you decide to intervene, what is the most appropriate action to take? (You may feel that more than one of the following possibilities are appropriate.)
   a. Call the student in for a conference.
   b. Ask the student's advisor to find out what the problem is.
   c. Ask the department chair to find out what the problem is.
   d. Refer the student to the counseling center.
   e. Refer the student to the office of students with disabilities.
4. Would your answer be any different if the student were:
   a. on a varsity athletic team and at risk of losing eligibility to play if he or she failed your course?
   b. sometimes seen sobbing or visibly upset at the beginning of class?
   c. previously a very successful student in your introductory course?
   d. the child of a colleague in the department?
   e. physically challenged in some way?
   f. a new transfer student for whom your course is his or her introduction to your college or university?
   g. a working non-traditional student who only takes one class at a time, and this term the course he or she is taking is yours?

Resolution

You decide that your first step will be to ask the student to come and see you for an informal conversation. When the student arrives at your office, you say, "I can't help but notice that your work to date in my courses hasn't been at the level that either of us would want. I'd like to help you if I can. Is there anything you can tell me about why your performance so far hasn't been very successful?"

At first the student simply repeats, "I just don't get it." But patiently, by asking follow-up questions and working through some of the textbook questions with the students, you begin to recognize a few specific areas of challenge. You try explaining concepts in a different way from how you described them in class, ask the student about other courses he or she has taken (so as to relate your material wherever possible to his or her prior learning), and recommend the six success strategies outlined in this chapter.

In particular, you talk about some of the resources the institution has available to help the student if factors other than the coursework itself are creating challenges. You express your openness to help as much as you can and, even though you know that this one student could end up occupying more of your time than all the others combined, you renew your commitment to do everything in your power to help promote student success.

FOR REFLECTION

Many students who struggle in their academic work report that they see each assignment, requirement, and course as just an obstacle to get out of the way. It's as though they're running a race: "I've got the math hurdle out of the way. Next I have to get over the English hurdle, then a few more hurdles in my major, and I can finally get my degree." They view the degree, not the learning that the degree represents, as the goal of college.

A major reason why they feel this way is that they don't understand *why* we are asking them to complete the assignments, requirements, and courses that we include in our programs. In order to engage students for greater success, college professors can begin by explaining, not just *what* they want students to achieve but *why* those goals are important. We can argue that it's not our job to motivate students; it's our job to teach them, and they should come to us already motivated. But the truth is that college professors who are committed to student success view their responsibility as lighting the lamp of understanding *and* fanning the flames that can transform their students from mere degree-seekers to fully engaged lifelong learners.

③

FACILITATING COLLEGIALITY
WITH OTHER FACULTY MEMBERS

One of the most important contributions a university can make is to provide a collegial and supportive environment in which students can learn and college professors can work. Collegiality among members of a program, unit, and institution is important because faculty members interact with their peers so frequently. If this contact stems from a spirit of professionalism and mutual respect, work as a college professor can be an overwhelmingly positive experience. If, on the other hand, interactions with other faculty members are characterized by rudeness, hostility, and contempt, teaching suffers, research becomes far more difficult, and service becomes a burden rather than a welcome opportunity to contribute to the greater community.

Some programs, recognizing the merits of promoting a collegial and civil environment, have developed statements that reflect their commitment to these principles. One example of such a statement is the following:

> The ABC Department at XYZ University is committed to providing a positive environment for all members of its community. Threatening language and/or actions will not be tolerated, and breaches of professional conduct will be handled swiftly and appropriately. The goal of our department is

to encourage all members to treat one another with respect and dignity within a safe and healthy environment.

Although these policies certainly send the right message, the verdict on their overall effectiveness has not yet been decided. Working as a faculty member at a college or university has changed tremendously over the past several decades. Today's faculty members often report that they're more stressed, exhausted by repeated pleas to "do more with less," anxious because of what appear to be ever-increasing expectations for promotion and tenure, concerned about the declining prestige of their profession, and convinced that far too many students are not adequately motivated or prepared for college. When the tense political environments that exist in many programs are added to this mix, it is no wonder that many college professors find their relationship with their colleagues to be strained. They feel they have barely enough energy to do their jobs, much less worry about how their words and actions may be perceived by others. The result is that many faculty members believe that institutions of higher education try to fulfill their missions with all the efficiency of the Department of Motor Vehicles and all the compassion of the Internal Revenue Service.

In their survey of faculty members, the authors asked respondents to speak about their experiences with collegiality—or the lack of it—in their academic programs. The result was surprising, even to two professionals who work with many institutions to help them develop more collegial, positive environments. When people were asked whether they had ever had a faculty member in their department (or other academic unit) whom they considered to be non-collegial, *100 percent* of the respondents—every single person who was surveyed—said yes. If you consider how difficult it can be to get people in a faculty meeting to agree on *anything*, the truly remarkable nature of that response becomes clear. Everyone the authors contacted could think of a case where professional collegiality had been a problem, and that result alone suggests the true severity of this problem.

Where there was a good deal less agreement was in the area of how to address these breaches in collegiality. The authors asked the group of college professors, "If there were an objective, validated instrument that measured collegial behavior, would you be in favor of having collegiality as a criterion for personnel decisions?"

- Almost half, 47 percent, said they'd prefer that collegiality be considered as part of the three criteria most commonly used today—teaching, research, and service—when personnel decisions are made.
- A lesser number, 29.4 percent, said they'd be in favor of collegiality being considered a fourth criterion in addition to teaching, research, and service.
- Even fewer, 11.7 percent, said they didn't believe that collegiality should be a criterion in personnel decisions at all.
- And the remaining respondents either did not answer the question or split their answers among such options as "I am uncertain" or "Other."

When these responses are combined, it's clear that most people would like collegiality addressed *somehow*: 73.4 percent of the faculty members we surveyed wanted it to be included as a factor in personnel decisions either by itself or in terms of its impact on other aspects of a faculty member's performance. The key is to be able to do so fairly, consistently, and as objectively as possible.

One piece of good news is that, given the right tools in their toolbox, college professors can make a positive difference in the collegiality of their units. Here are a few actions you can take to improve the climate of the environment where you work and increase the number of positive interactions you have with your colleagues.

- *Be proactive.* The best time to talk with others about issues of collegiality is *before* problems arise. Suggest that a few minutes be set aside at a faculty retreat or department meeting for everyone in attendance to discuss what collegiality means to them, why it's important, and how they believe breaches in collegiality should be addressed.
- *Model collegial behavior to others.* Toxic environments can be created when faculty members respond uncivilly to someone else's uncivil remark. You don't have to be a doormat and let other people walk all over you, but answering a negative and non-collegial remark with a positive and collegial response can break a cycle that might otherwise progress into a situation that benefits no one.

- *Don't allow incivility to pass without notice.* If you allow a breach of collegiality to stand without challenging it, you may inadvertently be giving others the impression that you condone and approve of what happened. In keeping with the previous principle, you don't want to be uncivil in your handling of the situation, but it can be very effective to say something like, "Excuse me, but I think that was a bit harsh and unnecessary. Perhaps what you actually meant to say was . . . "
- *Consult your supervisor, when necessary.* Reporting to the chair or dean every snipe and unflattering remark one faculty member ever said about another is just tattling and probably will be counterproductive. But in cases where breaches of collegiality are particularly egregious or ongoing, have a conversation about them with your supervisor. He or she may not be aware of how bad the situation has become and may be grateful to know how stakeholders of all kinds are being treated.

SCENARIO 3.1

You are a tenured full professor in a program where one of your colleagues, Dr. Narcissus N. Bully, is well known for his rude and intimidating remarks to members of the faculty, staff, and student body. One day you witness Dr. Bully addressing a tenure-track faculty member who only joined your program the year before. Dr. Bully's remarks are not merely condescending, they're also very personal, offensive, and very loud. The exchange is occurring in a hallway where students and other faculty members are also present.

Challenge Question:

What do you do?

Scenario Outcome:

Your status as a tenured full professor carries with it certain protections but also certain responsibilities. Among the protections it provides is that, although Dr. Bully can make an interaction with you unpleasant, there's relatively little he can do that will have a detrimental effect on your career. The untenured junior faculty member is far more vulnerable, however. That's why your status also carries with it an obligation to help your colleague.

You intervene and say to the junior faculty member, "Why don't you go to your office and start preparing for your next class? We can continue this conversation, perhaps, sometime when Dr. Bully has had a chance to calm down." The junior faculty member leaves, and your intervention causes Dr. Bully to redirect his wrath toward you.

"How dare you interrupt a private conversation like that? That was a stupid, unconscionable thing to do to a colleague, and I won't tolerate it. I'm filing a complaint with the department chair immediately."

"Absolutely. In fact, let's go see the chair right now." You keep your voice low and temper the anger that you feel. "The non-collegial act was what you were doing to our new faculty member. I intervened for your sake as much as for the other person. You were on the verge of saying things that would be completely destructive to our program. And what you may not realize is how much outbursts like that damage your own image with students and your colleagues. Now let's either go to an office where we can continue this conversation in private or do as you suggest and go see the chair of the department."

"This is a free country, and I have a right to say whatever I want to whomever I want however I want," Dr. Bully counters. "I have a right to be my own person."

"You're correct that you have a right to be yourself," you reply, "but that right stops when you start interfering with the rights of others. Each of our colleagues has a right to work in a collegial environment, free from intimidation, abuse, and bullying. In light of the public statements our dean has made about our need as educators to do what we can to stop bullying in schools, I'm sure she'll be rather displeased to learn that a senior member of her own faculty regularly bullies the most vulnerable of his colleagues. Now, shall we go have that talk with our chair?"

"Never mind!" Dr. Bully snorts and pushes past you on the way to his office. You decide that maybe it's time to have that talk about bullying with the department chair anyway, even if Dr. Bully has chosen not to participate.

SCENARIO 3.2

Imagine that you are the untenured junior faculty member in the previous scenario, but this time no one comes to your aid.

Challenge Question:

What do you do?

Scenario Outcome:

Dr. Bully has caught you off-guard in a public place, so you were completely unprepared for this encounter. After several sentences, however, you see where this conversation is headed. You interrupt Dr. Bully, being assertive but as calm as possible under the circumstances.

You say, "This is not the place for a conversation of this kind and, as your colleague, I have a right to be addressed with professionalism and respect. I'm not going to continue this conversation with you under these circumstances. Let's go together to the department chair's office, and you can outline your concerns, if you like, with a mediator present." Without waiting for a response, you head toward the chair's office.

"Don't you dare walk away from me!" Dr. Bully bellows. "You get back here!"

You continue walking but turn your head so that Dr. Bully can hear you, and say, "As I told you, I'm going to speak with the chair about what just happened. You can join me or not, as you wish." And, as promised, you proceed to the chair's office to recount the incident.

CASE STUDY 3.1: DR. MARGARITA DOBLE IS MY COLLEAGUE

When you joined the faculty in your first full-time position two years ago, a colleague, Dr. Margarita Doble, was hired at the same time. You have a cordial relationship with everyone in the program, including Dr. Doble. Your department chair is a highly respected scholar who has been very supportive of you ever since your arrival.

One of the peculiarities you've noticed about Dr. Doble is that she's very unpredictable. She can be talkative and jovial one minute, quiet and almost sullen the next. You haven't been too concerned about this inconsistency, however, chalking it up to one of those personality quirks we all have.

This semester, you and Dr. Doble happen both to have classes in adjoining rooms each Thursday evening. Because of your similar schedule, you noticed that she was late for class on several occasions. Moreover, when you happened to run into her during a break one week, her appearance didn't have its usual polish. Her hair was a mess, she was perspiring heavily, several fingernails had noticeable chips, and her outfit seemed a mismatch of colors and patterns. This appearance struck you as odd because Dr. Doble had always seemed to you to be a very stylish dresser who was almost vain about her appearance. Also unusual was the fact that she was chewing gum, something that you'd never known her to do previously.

On the way to the parking lot after class, you overhear several students talking about Dr. Doble's class. "Did you see how drunk she was?" one says. "She was slurring so badly I could hardly understand a word she was saying," another adds. "I thought she was going to keel over that one time," a third student says.

The students' comments disturb you enough that, as Dr. Doble's colleague, you feel a responsibility to do something. You know a few students who are in her classes this year and, over coffee that afternoon, you ask them how the course is going. At first the students are noncommittal but, after some prompting, they begin to open up. Among the things they tell you are the following.

- Dr. Doble is a really nice person, and they like her a lot, but she sometimes comes to class smelling of liquor.
- The night class this semester has been, in the students' opinion, "a disaster." She repeats the same concepts over and over, doesn't tie ideas together, and can take weeks to return papers and tests.
- In another course, one student says that Dr. Doble sometimes "goes off on a rant that," in the student's opinion, "really has nothing to do with the class."

- "We don't want to get Dr. Doble fired," another student says, "but we don't want our education ruined by a drunk either."

After what you witnessed the night before and heard from these few students, you decide that, since Dr. Margarita Doble is your colleague, you need to do something to help her—and the program.

Questions

1. Merely on the basis of what you know so far, what do you believe you should do?
2. What is likely to be the result if you do one of the following?
   a. You do nothing at all.
   b. You meet with Dr. Doble and share only your own firsthand observations.
   c. You meet with Dr. Doble and share the remarks you heard from your students.
   d. You tell the department chair about what you have learned through observation and your meeting with students.
   e. You tell the dean, the director of human resources, your chair, and the university attorney about what you have learned through observation and your meeting with students.
   f. You call a meeting with Dr. Doble and your chair, confronting Dr. Doble with the information and perception you have gathered.
3. Would your response be any different if one of the following were true?
   a. If, instead of being a relatively new, untenured faculty member, you were a tenured full professor
   b. If Dr. Doble were a tenured full professor, while you were an untenured junior faculty member
   c. If instead of being a stylish dresser, Dr. Doble had always been rather careless about her appearance
   d. If you hadn't overheard the students speaking in the parking lot after class
   e. If instead of Dr. Margarita Doble, the protagonist of this story were a male colleague, Dr. Jose Cuervo

   f. If instead of Dr. Doble, the protagonist of this story were Dr.
      Bully from the scenarios earlier in this chapter
4. Do you believe that the name Dr. Margarita Doble (or Dr. Jose
   Cuervo) may have colored your impressions of what occurred in
   any way?

Resolution

You're sufficiently concerned about Dr. Doble that you decide to
share your thoughts with the department chair. As it turned out, this
isn't the first time that a similar concern has been raised about Dr.
Doble. The chair thus has you write down what you observed yourself
along with what the students told you and takes this document to a
meeting with the dean and director of human resources.

You don't hear anything more about the incident for several days. You
assume that some type of investigation is going on to determine whether
your concerns are warranted. Finally, late on a Friday afternoon, the
chair asks you to drop by the office. When you arrive, you notice that
the dean is also there.

"Let me bring you up to date on what has happened," the chair begins.
"Based on your written statement and similar concerns I'd heard before, I
met with Dr. Doble along with a representative of the union. I mentioned
your concerns—I tried to keep your name out of it, but I'm afraid she fig-
ured it out almost immediately from the context—and similar allegations
I'd heard from other faculty members. We talked about the Employee Assistance Program, which can provide help with substance abuse problems,
and the director of human resources then joined us. I said that participation in an alcohol abuse program would be a requirement of her con-
tinued employment and had our union representative confirm that this
provision was in accordance with the collective bargaining agreement."

"Well, that's good," you say. "At least she's getting help. That's the
important thing. I wanted to be a good colleague."

"Wait," the chair continues. "There's more. The next morning, Dr.
Doble showed up in the dean's office with her attorney. They brought a
signed affidavit from her doctor stating that Dr. Doble is a severe diabetic,
and all the things you were observing—mood swings, disorientation,

confusion, heavy perspiration, a fruity or acetone scent, dizziness, and everything else—are symptoms of her condition.

"She's filing a lawsuit for defamation against the institution—and against you, I'm afraid. She said that if you had bothered to ask or even if you'd ever noticed the medical identification bracelet she always wore, you wouldn't have been so non-collegial as to make allegations that humiliated her, cost her unneeded expense, and jeopardized her reputation with her students. Since your statements went above and beyond your professional duties at the institution, the office of legal affairs will only be protecting the university, but not you personally. Frankly, I'd advise you to retain legal counsel."

Reflection

Now go back and read through the case study again, noting any words that, if given due attention, may have prevented you from taking the action described in the Resolution section.

THE IMPORTANCE OF COLLEGIALITY

In their surveys to college professors, the authors asked respondents to identify how important they thought collegiality was relative to six other major qualifications, skills, or attributes. The factors people were asked to rank in significance were:

- teaching
- research
- service
- collegiality
- vision
- organizational skills
- success in receiving grants

When those taking the survey were asked about how important these factors were for their fellow *faculty members*, collegiality ranked second in importance only to teaching. Priority order for college professors was as follows:

1. Teaching (82.3 percent of respondents ranked it number one in importance; 99.8 percent placed it in their top three most important factors.)
2. Collegiality (11.7 percent ranked it as number one in importance; 64.5 percent ranked it in the top three.)
3. Research (17.6 percent ranked it as number one in importance; 52.8 percent ranked it in the top three.)
4. Service (5.8 percent ranked it as number one in importance; 46.9 percent ranked it in the top three.)
5. Organizational skills (5.8 percent ranked it as number one in importance; 35.1 percent ranked it in the top three.)
6. Success in receiving grants (0 percent ranked it as number one in importance, 17.5 percent ranked it in the top three.)
7. Vision (0 percent ranked it as number one in importance; 5.8 percent ranked in the top three.)

In other words, most faculty members consider collegiality as a more important quality in their peers than research, service, or anything else that is generally regarded as a key to faculty success.

When the focus turned from faculty members to department chairs and deans, respondents to the survey ranked the same seven qualifications, skills, or attributes in a somewhat different order. For *department chairs*, no matter how the data was analyzed, the seven factors were always ranked as:

1. Organizational skills
2. Collegiality
3. Vision
4. Teaching
5. Service
6. Success in receiving grants
7. Research

For *deans*, the order of priority became:

1. Vision
2. Organizational skills
3. Collegiality

4. Teaching
5. Service
6. Success in receiving grants
7. Research

What we can conclude from this survey is how important college professors regard collegiality to be both for their peers and for administrators
alike. Regardless of the group under consideration, collegiality *always*
outranked research, service, and success in receiving grants, the three
factors that many evaluation systems tend to emphasize.

It's a fallacy, therefore, to think that strong, top-down leadership is
the most effective way to run a college or a university. Regardless of
whether the topic is faculty leadership or administrative effectiveness,
the vast majority of college professors say that they respond more favorably to collegial, people-oriented leaders than to tough, results-oriented
leaders.

CASE STUDY 3.2: "HOUSTON, WE HAVE A (MORALE) PROBLEM"

You are a tenured full professor who recently returned to teaching after
having chaired your department for twelve years. During your term as
chair, you played a key role in hiring nearly every other member of the
department, including the person who is now serving as chair. One of
the principles you tried to follow in faculty searches could best be summarized as "hire for attitude and train for skill." As a result, you're very
proud of your colleagues in the program: They're not only excellent
teachers and accomplished scholars but also caring, supportive, and professional in all their interactions with students, faculty, and staff alike.

Because of an economic downturn, your institution has recently been
strapped for resources. Budget cuts were relatively minor at first, but
for the past two years have become truly severe. For many years the
contractual teaching load had been the equivalent of three courses a semester, with most faculty members teaching two because their research
assignment, thesis supervision, or service responsibilities were treated
as substitutes for their third course. When you were chair, you taught

one course a semester. One of your colleagues served as undergraduate coordinator and received an additional course reduction for this assignment. Another colleague played a similar role as graduate coordinator and received a comparable reduction in teaching duties. Throughout your term as chair, you developed other creative ways of lightening the teaching load of faculty members in the department. For example, you appointed one faculty member to be a community outreach liaison, another to be a faculty development coordinator, and a third to head up the discipline's efforts in fundraising and grant writing.

From your perspective, this approach had numerous benefits: Instruction was excellent because faculty members had plenty of time to prepare their courses; student retention was high because the undergraduate and graduate coordinators could address small problems before they became large challenges; external funding gave your program additional resources; and research productivity was among the best at the institution.

The recent series of budget cuts has, however, threatened to undermine all these accomplishments. There has been a hiring freeze. Research and travel funds have been greatly reduced. Salary increases have been non-existent. And enrollment caps have been raised in all courses. The outlook for the current year appears even worse: The president and provost have told faculty members to be prepared for an additional 10 percent budget cut on top of the reductions that have already been made. Public resistance to the cost of college has made the idea of a tuition increase impossible. Efforts to enroll a large number of international students, who are expected to pay full tuition but often have academic challenges because of their limited proficiencies in English, may cause class sizes to grow even further.

Worst of all, the upper administration has made a unilateral decision to increase the teaching load of the faculty from three to four courses a semester and to eliminate all reassignments from teaching to other duties. As a result, most faculty members in your discipline will see their loads jump from two courses a semester to four courses, without any consideration given to their responsibilities in other areas. Untenured faculty members will be hit particularly hard: Since expectations for research have risen significantly in recent years, they'll now be expected to endure high teaching and service obligations while still producing refereed articles, successful grant proposals, patents, and creative scholarly works.

As expected, morale plunges throughout the institution, but it's particularly bad in your department because of how good matters were while you were chair. Your formerly congenial faculty now quarrels openly in department meetings as each person believes that he or she is being treated more unfairly than anyone else. A vote of no confidence is taken against the new chair who is being blamed (unfairly in your opinion) for circumstances that couldn't have been foreseen.

What was supposed to be a weekly meeting to discuss a proposed change to your department's degree requirements swiftly descends into chaos. People treat the chair with a mixture of anger and contempt. They say that they'll refuse to continue fulfilling the non-teaching assignments they've been given since they'll no longer receive release time for them. Nothing productive is being accomplished, and it pains you to see faculty members, who were once so supportive of their colleagues, now openly turn on one another.

Questions

1. What, if anything, could you do to improve this situation?
2. To what extent do you feel responsible for the current problem by making so many reassignments from teaching duties?
3. What is likely to be the result if you took any of the following actions?
   a. You let the current chair handle the problem since this person is now in charge.
   b. You come strongly to the defense of the new chair and make it clear to the others that he or she is doing the best that can be done under very difficult circumstances.
   c. You form a common cause with your colleagues and support their desire to stop performing any service to the discipline for which they don't receive additional compensation.
   d. You tell the chair that the current situation has no positive outcome and that he or she should resign in order to allow the discipline to have a new beginning.

e. You tell the current chair to resign and offer to assume the role of chair again yourself.

f. You meet one-on-one with the department chair to develop strategies for the department to follow in the face of this crisis.

g. You raise your voice in the meeting and tell your colleagues to sit down, stop arguing, and discuss the matter rationally and calmly.

h. You work behind the scenes to get a group of students to write letters to the president, provost, and governing board, protesting the effect of these budget cuts on their educations.

4. Would your response be any different if any of the following were true?

a. If student enrollment were increasing throughout the institution but declining in your discipline

b. If the president and chair of the governing board had made public remarks disparaging your discipline as "outdated" and "not suitable for today's job market"

c. If you and the current chair were the only members of the discipline with tenure

Resolution

You come to the defense of the chair in the faculty meeting, which eventually comes to an unsatisfactory and unproductive end. Later that day, you visit the chair to discuss various ways the situation in the department might be improved. Eventually the two of you agree on a strategy.

The chair will call a special meeting to address the concerns that were brought up by various members of the faculty. However, the chair will ask that you be allowed to run the meeting since you're still regarded as an "honest broker" by most of the people who will be in attendance. When it's your turn to speak, you'll talk candidly about the current budget crisis and lead a discussion about the possibility of offering fewer services than the faculty had provided in the past since their teaching load has now increased and extra compensation isn't possible.

The two of you follow this plan, and the meeting is set for the beginning of the following week. After a thorough discussion of what it would mean to cut back on services, however, the faculty decides that this approach wouldn't be in their best interests. The result would harm the students and the program, probably lead to reduced enrollments, and not be effective at expressing the department's displeasure at the way the upper administration has imposed the budget reduction.

As a result, the faculty votes unanimously not to take any action that would not be to the advantage of the students. Instead, there will be a complete re-examination of workload to make sure that responsibilities are shared equitably. One new idea is to move undergraduate students in their first year or two in the program from individual to group advising sessions: At this point in the program, the students' requirements are all largely the same, and group advising will take less time while still permitting more extensive mentoring of upper division and graduate students.

The chair agrees to focus that year's fundraising efforts on securing support for endowed faculty lines, work-study students, staff advisors, and other measures that can help alleviate the increase in faculty workload. What had started as a very tense meeting ends on a surprisingly positive note as people feel that they are all working together again collegially in order to achieve a shared goal.

CASE STUDY 3.3: A COLLEGE COLLEAGUE WHO IS NOT COLLEGIAL

You're a tenured professor in a department of nine full-time faculty members. Six of your colleagues, including the department chair, are tenured and two are not. This year you are chairing the Department Evaluation Committee (DEC) and, in this capacity, you serve along with two other tenured faculty members in your department.

The roles and responsibilities of the DEC are to review the portfolios of faculty who are being considered for reappointment, tenure, promotion, or post-tenure review and to make a recommendation to the department chair about the decision to be made in the case of each candidate. The DEC has historically been a very powerful committee: Throughout your time in the department, you've never known its recommendation to be overturned.

A few of the reasons why your department's DEC has been so highly regarded by the chair, as well as the dean and the upper administration, are that the membership of the committee has always been elected through a unanimous vote, the group hasn't shied away from making tough decisions, and the reasons for its recommendations have always been clear and well documented. During an untenured faculty member's probationary period, the DEC reviews that person's performance each year and recommends that a contract either be offered for the following year or that a letter of non-reappointment be prepared. All personnel decisions must give attention to the standard three parts of the academic triad: teaching, research, and service.

One of the department's two untenured assistant professors, Dr. Snootessa N. Callous ("Snooty" for short) graduated from a very prestigious university and did a post-doc at a major European research institute. Everyone in the program is well aware of these achievements because Snooty regularly mentions them within the first few minutes of any conversation. In her first three years, Dr. Callous has produced three referred articles in first-tier journals and an essay in *The Atlantic* magazine, and she was featured as a rising star in *The Chronicle of Higher Education*.

Despite these achievements, Dr. Callous's teaching evaluations are as bimodal as any you've ever seen: Students either adore or detest her; there appears to be no middle ground. When, as part of your duties, you and the other members of the DEC were going to observe one of her classes, Dr. Callous kept coming up with excuses why "today won't work": "I'm giving a test," "Students are making reports for the entire period," "Only a few people will be there today, and your presence would ruin the activity I've got planned."

Later you heard Dr. Callous speak disparagingly of you to someone on the phone, calling you "this idiot who keeps trying to invade my class." When you confront her with what you overheard, Dr. Callous responds angrily and tells you that it's a violation of her academic freedom as an internationally acclaimed scholar to have you "destroy the carefully designed learning atmosphere" she has been able to create. Nevertheless, as chair of the DEC, you insist that it is appropriate for you and your colleagues to observe her course and show her the policy that enables you to do so. Grudgingly and with barely concealed contempt, she finally says that you can come to class this Wednesday "if you insist."

When Wednesday comes, you and the other members of the DEC are expecting the worst. But to your surprise, the class is actually quite wonderful. Dr. Callous got all of her students actively engaged, and you were impressed by how quickly they grasped a concept that you yourself always had difficulty explaining. Dr. Callous was even quite gracious when one of the students slipped and called her "Snooty": Rather than demonstrating offense, she turned the occasion into a teaching moment about how conventions sometimes change in different environments and proceeded with the class.

You are so impressed, in fact, that afterward you feel you simply have to tell Dr. Callous how well the class had gone. You get a few words out of your mouth, but Dr. Callous simply looks right through you as though you're not even there and walks away.

As you prepare for your meeting with the DEC, you are reminded of a few other aspects to Dr. Callous's behavior. She has no friends or even close colleagues within the department or anywhere else at the institution as far as you know. She doesn't socialize with other professors: You know of several parties, campus events, and departmental celebrations she's been invited to, but she's never bothered to RSVP or attend them. She attends all department meetings, as required by contract, but has little or nothing to contribute. On those very few occasions when she did interact with another faculty member, she either corrected the person about a very minor error or cited one of her own successes.

You finally come to the conclusion that you simply don't like Dr. Snootessa N. Callous. Apparently you're not alone in this judgment: Many faculty members go out of their way to avoid her, and no one ever says anything positive about her. She does serve on two departmental and two university-wide committees. She is always present for all of the meetings of the committees.

When the DEC meets, one of the other members notes that the committee has recommended to Dr. Callous each year that she take steps to improve her interpersonal behavior toward other members of the program. As a result, this member proposes that Dr. Callous be recommended for a letter of non-reappointment. The other member disagrees, saying, "Look, she's entitled to her own personality. The fact remains that she *is* a superstar. It's not bragging if what you say is true. And with her publications and contacts throughout the discipline, she could put this department on the map. Besides, her teaching was great, and you know it." It looks as though for the first time the DEC's recommendation won't be unanimous, and the final decision is up to you.

QUESTIONS

1. Based only on what you know so far, what are you inclined to do?
2. What is likely to be the result if you took one of the following actions?
   a. You voted to recommend that Dr. Callous's contract not be renewed.
   b. You voted to recommend that Dr. Callous's contract be renewed but included a statement that she needed to work on her interpersonal relations.
   c. You voted to recommend that Dr. Callous's contract be renewed but included a warning that she was unlikely to be recommended for tenure unless her behavior toward other members of the faculty improved.
   d. You insisted that the DEC meet jointly with the chair to discuss the best way to proceed.
   e. You insisted that the DEC meet jointly with all tenured members of the discipline to discuss the best way to proceed.
3. Would your decision be different if any of the following were true?
   a. If Dr. Callous were the only female member of the department in its history
   b. If Dr. Callous were a member of an ethnic minority
   c. If Dr. Callous were the recipient of a large federal grant, the overhead from which the department depended on for supplementing its budget
   d. If this were not Dr. Callous's third year but the last year before a tenure decision would be made
   e. If budget cuts made it almost inevitable that if Dr. Callous were not renewed, the program would lose that much-needed faculty line
   f. If the institution had a policy explicitly stating that collegiality could be considered in matters of contract renewal and tenure

Resolution

You try very hard to separate your personal feelings from what you believe to be fair and appropriate. On the one hand, there is documented evidence that Dr. Callous was instructed to improve her interpersonal relations with other members of the program in each of the DEC's previous recommendations. On the other, she at least has the capacity to be an excellent teacher (to judge by the class you observed), is building a superb record of publications, and appears to be a highly regarded scholar. You try to put reason ahead of your gut feeling and vote to recommend that her contract be renewed. The result is the first split vote that the DEC has given in its history.

Due to this lack of unanimity, the department chair doesn't simply accept the committee's recommendation. The chair discusses the matter with other members of the department, meets with the dean, and acts jointly with the dean to give Dr. Callous a letter of non-reappointment. You can only imagine how she acted when she received the letter. At any rate, when you come in the following Monday, you discover that she has cleaned out her office and accepted a longstanding offer from Esteemed International University to head a new research initiative there. Since she has walked out before the end of the academic year, you and your colleagues are forced to cover her classes.

Over the next several years, you follow Snooty's career with great interest. She is the recipient of a number of large international grants, publishes books that are popular not merely with academics but with the reading public as well, is frequently mentioned as a contender for a Nobel Prize, and brings remarkable acclaim to Esteemed International University. You continue to wonder whether your own institution made a terrible mistake in her case or, in the dean's words, "dodged a bullet on that one."

THE CONCEPT OF POSITIVE DEFAULT

The expression *default mode* is used to describe anything that exists in its normal or unaltered state. For example, we might purchase a software program that regularly saves our work every five minutes unless we alter the settings so as to make this automatic activity either more or less frequent. The five-minute setting is thus that software's default mode. But people have default modes just as do electronic devices and software applications. Some people naturally trust others unless they have reason to feel otherwise. Other people are naturally suspicious of those they meet until they believe their trust has been earned. In either case, this level of trust or suspicion is that person's default mode of interpersonal relations.

When we have difficult interactions with others, it's very common to lapse into *negative default*: the assumption that the other person is creating problems because he or she is flawed, misguided, or immoral. But as college professors, we're often more successful in our interpersonal relations when we choose to adopt a *positive default*: the assumption that the vast majority of people are really just trying to do what's best, even if we may at times disagree with their methods or intentions. Consciously adopting a positive default (sometimes also known as *positive bias*) can be an important step toward facilitating collegiality with other faculty members.

If you find yourself naturally adopting a negative default in challenging situations, resetting your tendency to think the worst of others can feel awkward and unnatural at first. But you can begin altering your default mode by asking yourself the following questions whenever you're tempted to think that a person is causing trouble simply because "that's just how the person is":

- Is it reasonable to assume that another person would ever think, "I know what would constitute good behavior in this circumstance, and I am choosing to do something bad instead?" If that is not a reasonable sequence of thoughts, why do I assume that others have them?
- Don't most people really want what's best for themselves and others?
- When I made a mistake or caused other people trouble in the past, was I intentionally trying to be a bad person? If I don't act that way, why would I assume that others would?
- Is it reasonable to assume that one of my colleagues would *not* want what's best for himself or herself, our students, our program, and our institution?

Once we start to realize that other people are really trying to do their best, even though we may have disagreements with them about what "the best" is or how to achieve it, we're much more likely to see how it's possible to resolve our differences and move forward. After all, a mistake can be fixed; a bad or corrupt person can seem impossible to deal with.

SCENARIO 3.3

You regard yourself as a friendly, easygoing person, and thus you get along with the vast majority of your colleagues. That majority does not, however, include Dr. Ruth Lessogre who, for whatever reason, took an instant dislike to you from the moment you joined the faculty, and her opinion of you has only declined ever since.

Dr. Lessogre's treatment of you often just seems mean-spirited. When it was announced at a faculty meeting that your tenure application was successful, she was the only member of the department who didn't congratulate you. When you speak on committees where Dr. Lessogre is present, she rolls her eyes and appears to become fascinated with her text messages. She held an end-of-the-year party last spring; you weren't invited. You sent her a congratulatory note when her grant was funded; she never acknowledged it. When your book came out, you sent everyone in the program a personally autographed copy; you later found the copy you sent her in the trash.

When you ask a colleague in another department about why Dr. Lessogre seems to treat you so poorly, you're told, "Oh, that's just who she is. She's a spiteful, insufferable, vindictive person. I wouldn't take it personally. She probably hates everybody."

Challenge Question:

Should you take you colleague's advice and assume that you just can't please everyone, or is it worth trying to improve your relationship with Dr. Lessogre?

Scenario Outcome:

Initially you assume that your colleague is correct and Dr. Lessogre must just be a mean-spirited person. Now that you have tenure, she can't do much to harm you, so why not just avoid her and get on with your life? But then you realize that you're lapsing into negative default and that your assessment of Dr. Lessogre is actually somewhat unreasonable. Does it really make sense to think that certain people are just so filled with hostility and anger that they'd hate someone for no reason at all? You decide that this conclusion really doesn't seem very logical and that you're not quite ready to give up on Dr. Lessogre.

You notice that Dr. Lessogre holds office hours from 2:00 to 4:00 p.m. every Thursday. Shortly after 2:00 the next Thursday, you show up at Dr. Lessogre's office, verify that no students are waiting to see her, and try to initiate a conversation by saying, "I just can't help but notice that there's this wall of hostility between us." You cite a few of the less severe examples of how Dr. Lessogre has treated you, taking care not to seem accusatorial when you describe them. "I can't understand why this is the case because I have so much respect for you. I admire your research greatly, and when I have your students in my classes, I'm always so impressed by how much they've gained from your courses."

At first, Dr. Lessogre is noncommittal and pretends not to know what you're talking about. She says she's busy and needs you to leave her office. You acknowledge her concerns but continue gently to explore what you may have done to have earned such ill will. Finally, after prolonging the conversation for over an hour, you hear Dr. Lessogre refer to the "flawed search process" that resulted in your hiring. With a few more questions, you discover that Dr. Lessogre had a friend who was also a finalist for that position and, in Dr. Lessogre's mind (though not apparently in the view of the rest of the department), was better qualified and working in a more exciting area of the discipline.

Rather than becoming defensive, you say, "You know, I can understand that. Loyalty to friends is important, and searches don't always go the way we want them, too. Thank you for being open with me, and I'd like eventually to demonstrate to you the value that I think I'm bringing to this program." You leave Dr. Lessogre's office on slightly better terms than when you entered it. Although you don't expect that Dr. Lessogre will instantly become one of your strong supporters and friends, you believe that, by trusting your positive default, you're at least now on the right path.

FOR REFLECTION

As college professors, we place a great deal of emphasis on teaching, research, and service. But it's the relationship we have with others that often determines our level of job satisfaction and even the degree of success we achieve in our disciplines. Building a collegial environment takes a collected effort of everyone involved, but that effort can begin with a single individual. And there's no reason at all why that individual can't be you.

4

ESTABLISHING POSITIVE INTERACTIONS WITH ADMINISTRATORS

A common stereotype of administrators is that they're all penny-pinching, bean-counting tyrants who love nothing better than to stuff a college professor's class with as many students as possible and then proceed to reject every request for anything that could make the professor's job more palatable. While some administrators may well adhere to that rather unflattering picture, they're almost certainly in a very small minority. Most university administrators still view themselves as faculty members. They chose an academic profession because they care about scholarship and students. They do whatever they can to help other professors succeed, even when resources are few and demands are great.

At times, administrators may seem to be out of sync with professors because their responsibilities cause them to have a different perspective. As the title of a book by Robert Smith, the former provost and senior vice president at Texas Tech University, puts it, *Where You Stand Is Where You Sit* (2006). In other words, the positions we hold can often affect our outlook and values. What may appear to a professor as meddling and constantly raising course enrollments may appear to an administrator as a means of making sure that students get the courses they need while keeping the institution financially strong enough to avoid faculty layoffs.

This difference in perspective and values helps explain why professors and administrators sometimes appear to be speaking different languages. One of the best ways in which faculty members can help establish positive interactions with administrators, therefore, is to learn how to "translate" concepts from the viewpoint and principles of administrators to the viewpoint and principles of their colleagues and back again. We call this type of communication the *Babel fish approach* to communication after an idea developed by Douglas Adams in his 1979 novel *The Hitchhiker's Guide to the Galaxy*. Adams's fictitious Babel fish was a small, yellow creature that fed on brain energy. If you slipped one in your ear, you could instantly understand whatever someone said to you in any language.

The Babel fish approach to communication involves asking yourself six questions any time you're interacting with someone whose perspective is likely to be very different from yours.

1. What is it that I want to occur?
2. Why do I want it?
3. How are the reasons why I want it likely to be perceived by the other person?
4. What does the other person want to occur?
5. Why does he or she want it?
6. How could what I want be presented, not in terms of why I want it (particularly if those reasons are likely distasteful to or misunderstood by the other person), but as a means of getting closer to what that person wants?

For example, suppose you're trying to obtain funding to attend a conference from an administrator who's notoriously tight with the budget. The Babel fish approach might work something like the following.

1. What is it that I want to occur? I want to receive sufficient funding to attend the conference.
2. Why do I want it? It would be great to get some break from my standard routine, see some of my colleagues from graduate school, and learn a bit more about new developments in my field.
3. How are the reasons why I want it likely to be perceived by the other person? This administrator is likely to view this trip as a mere

junket and think that my reasons for wanting to attend the conference are all about what helps me and less about what benefits the program.

4. What does the other person want to occur? The administrator wants to keep spending to a minimum and to increase the number of students in our program who pay the full cost of their tuition.

5. Why does he or she want it? This administrator is under pressure to keep the entire unit within its budget and is evaluated on the extent to which that goal is achieved.

6. How could what I want be presented, not in terms of why I want it (particularly if those reasons are likely distasteful to or misunderstood by the other person), but as a means of getting closer to what that person wants? I should present this conference as an opportunity for me to recruit additional students in the area and to learn new strategies for lowering our technology costs in the program. The administrator won't be sympathetic to my desire for a break in routine and to see old friends, so this request should not be phrased as intended to achieve those goals.

Some people see the Babel fish approach and think, "I can't do that. I have to call it like I see it. It's dishonest to conceal your motives in this way." But the Babel fish approach isn't about creating *false* motives; it's about finding a way to present our goals as helping to achieve someone else's motives. It's the sort of thing that college professors do all the time when they write a grant proposal. They rarely find a funding agency that wants to support the exact project they'd like to work on. Instead they find a way of explaining how the project they want to pursue will help the funding agency achieve its goals. In essence, they're engaging in the Babel fish approach to communication.

CASE STUDY 4.1: SEEING MATTERS FROM THE PERSPECTIVE OF OTHERS

You're in desperate need of a new full-time faculty line for your program. Specifically, you don't have enough faculty members to meet course demand. You're afraid that, if you raise enrollment caps in your courses any further, course quality will deteriorate and even more of your colleagues will begin to accept positions elsewhere. (Three of the best professors in your department have already accepted other job offers over the past several years.) The committee load of the faculty at your institution is exceptionally high, and you believe that service and teaching commitments are occupying valuable time that members of the faculty should be devoting to their research. As a result, you're concerned that two of your junior colleagues may have a difficult time earning tenure when they are reviewed three years from now.

Using the Babel fish approach that we discussed in this chapter, how do you make a case for securing a new faculty line that is most likely to persuade each of the following people?

Your Dean

- Is a career academic who has never worked outside a university, is not much of a people person, and hates conflict
- Wants to promote: student success (which this person defines as high retention rates and timely graduation) and his or her own career
- Wants to avoid: conflict, fighting a battle that can't be won, and having to argue in favor of something that he or she really doesn't believe in

A Member of the Board of Trustees

- Is a no-nonsense, "just the facts," business-oriented person who believes that the only reason to go to college is to get a job
- Wants to promote: holding down tuition costs, increasing job placement rates for graduates, and the (positive) visibility of the university
- Wants to avoid: low productivity (which this person defines as professors doing anything other than teaching their classes) and bad publicity for the university

A Potential Donor

- Is very talkative—likes to socialize before getting down to business; easily distracted—gets "off-topic" frequently; somewhat "time intensive;" and considered "high maintenance"
- Wants to promote: the arts and culture, opportunities for the disadvantaged, and global health
- Wants to avoid: blunt requests for financial support, being rushed, and anything that he or she regards as "low class"

Questions

1. What would likely be the response from each of the three people mentioned in the case study—the dean, trustee, and potential donor—if you said that you needed the new position for each of the following reasons?
   a. "All of us in the department are just too overworked."
   b. "Our field is changing, and we need a specialist in this new, emerging specialty."
   c. "If we could offer a greater variety of classes, we might attract more majors."
   d. "In order to improve the quality of our courses, we need to decrease out student/faculty ratio."
   e. "None of us are ever able to take sabbaticals because we're just so understaffed."
   f. "If we don't fill this new position, more of our professors will probably go on the market."
   g. "If we don't fill this new position, I'll probably go on the market."
   h. "We can't meet course demand with our current staffing; we're turning students away every semester."
   i. "The university that's our biggest rival and competitor has more than twice as many faculty members in its department."
   j. "All of us on the faculty are just drowning in committee work; we don't have nearly enough time for research."
   k. "If we don't get this new position now, I think that two junior faculty members in the department won't qualify for tenure as a result of our current workload."
2. Based on what you know about the three people mentioned in the case study, where would you hold each conversation to increase the probability of your success?
   a. With any of these people, would a letter, memorandum, or email be more effective than a face-to-face conversation?
   b. With any of them, would it be effective to send a written proposal in advance of a face-to-face conversation?
3. Suppose that each of the people mentioned in this case study turned down your request. What would have to be different about

their response to make you decide to ask again later (perhaps with a different rationale) as opposed to considering the matter closed forever?

Resolution

You make an appointment with the dean and bring with you a proposal for a new position that lists your rationale in concise bullet points and that is accompanied by several graphs and tables of information. Your argument can be summarized as follows.

- Surveys of students who transfer from your institution to another school regularly list lack of course selection in your area as a primary reason for leaving.
- The schools to which they most often transfer have at least two more faculty members for every hundred students in the program than your department does, and that is why they are able to offer a broader range of courses than you are.
- Based on data gathered from programs similar to yours, you have calculated that, on the basis of tuition generated by new students who would be interested in the program if it offered more options, coupled with the tuition saved through increased student retention, the additional faculty line would not only cover its cost but would also generate a profit for the college.

The dean is intrigued by your argument but is hesitant to advocate for this new position strongly unless the president, governing board, and department chair are equally supportive. You mention that one of the trustees called you and invited you to lunch the following week to talk about your program. You ask the dean if you could discuss the possible new position with the trustee and gauge whether there is any support for increasing your program's staffing at that level of the institution. The dean gives you permission to proceed and, understanding that the dean isn't much of a people person, you wrap up the meeting quickly and leave.

The following week the trustee meets you for lunch and, almost as soon as you're seated, launches into a speech that you've heard often enough before: Too many students go to college without any clear understanding of why they're there; they take a lot of courses that they don't need and that don't benefit anyone; they graduate without any prospect of getting a job; and a college education should be short, practical, and much less expensive than it is now.

You don't answer these points directly but remark that one of the things you've always admired about the business this particular trustee has built was the value that the company provided its customers in all of its products. Even though other companies may have sold similar products for a lower price, those products didn't have as much value because they wore out and had to be replaced so quickly. The trustee is pleased that you're so familiar with the company and its business philosophy. In fact, your comment prompts a rather extended discourse by the trustee regarding how that business philosophy developed and why value is always a more reliable predictor of success than price alone.

"The same idea holds true of our academic program," you reply. You've brought with you several charts indicating your program's placement rates of its graduates in jobs and post-graduate programs over the past decade. You call the trustee's attention to how those placement rates are increasing and have the potential to increase even further with a very slight expansion in the course offerings you provide. You note that, in order to achieve that next level of success, you would need one new faculty position, and you describe the profile of the faculty member you'd be looking for. "As you said," you conclude, "value is often a far more important factor than cost. This new position would probably raise our cost slightly—although with better retention and increased enrollment, the cost per student credit hour produced would actually go down—but it will pay off in even better job placement rates as well as a great deal of positive publicity for the institution."

After further discussion, the trustee seems ready to support the creation of this new faculty position with the president and provost but urges you to explore other possibilities for funding the position as well. "As a matter of fact," you say, "I'm meeting with a potential donor in a few days, and I'm hoping that this conversation might eventually result in some external funding." The trustee encourages you to proceed with that approach, and the lunch concludes on a cordial note.

Several days later you drive to the potential donor's home and arrive promptly at the time agreed upon when the invitation was offered. You bring several small gifts, including a signed copy of a book written by one of your colleagues in the department and a framed photograph of the donor receiving an honorary degree from the institution several years previously. You're invited into a large, elegantly furnished sitting area where tea and small pastries are soon served.

For the better part of an hour, the two of you simply make light conversation. You talk about your families, the best Italian restaurants in the area, whether any of the university's athletic teams will have a chance at a championship next year, and how the area could really stand some rain. Eventually the potential donor brings up a favorite topic: how the local community really ought to be doing more to help the disadvantaged.

You express your agreement and note that it's precisely for this reason that you've been working on expanding your academic program. With the additional courses the department could provide by hiring one additional faculty member with the specialty you have in mind, you believe strongly that even more students—including those to which the university gives its generous scholarships and financial aid packages—could be placed in careers that could help their entire families. You refer to the data you've collected, but don't produce it since you sense that the donor's primary interest is in those disadvantaged students, not the statistics you have in the folder you brought.

You wonder aloud if the potential donor might have any advice about foundations or other funding sources that might be able to assist you with this goal, and you take out a small notebook, ready to write down anything your host recommends to you. Instead of answering, the conversation goes off on another tangent. But later as you're gathering your belongings and thanking the potential donor for a lovely afternoon, the topic suddenly shifts back to your desire for a new faculty position. "You know, I've been thinking about what you said before when we were talking about finding people jobs, and I think I can help. Let me know what it would cost to endow half of that new position you were talking about. If the university is willing to commit to the idea by funding half of it, I think I can manage to supply the other half."

You thank your host profusely and know that, with this commitment, you now have all the support you need to bring your dean and the trustee you met with fully on board with your proposal.

THE IMPORTANCE OF POSITIVE RELATIONS WITH ADMINISTRATORS

With all of the responsibilities you have as a college professor, why should you even care whether you maintain a positive relationship with college administrators? Without being too Machiavellian, we might answer this question by saying, "Because it's in your interest to do so." Department chairs, deans, provosts, and presidents have the authority to make decisions that can affect your career and have a major impact on your life. They can grant exceptions to policies that may be hindering you from attaining an important goal. They can provide additional funding for equipment, travel, and research expenses. And they have an important role in promotion and tenure decisions.

In a perfect world, it wouldn't really matter whether people liked you when a decision was being made about your promotion and tenure prospects. You'd simply be evaluated on your merits and nothing more. But the real world of academics is more complicated than that. Your merits matter, of course. They matter more than anything. But people who make decisions frequently find it difficult to separate how they feel about someone from whether they should act on that person's behalf. Often this process occurs subconsciously, but it does occur. For that reason, you may want to keep in mind what we call the **Buller/Cipriano Principle**: It's easier to say no to someone you don't like and harder to resist helping someone you do like.

Suppose, for example, that the institution is undergoing severe financial difficulties and has to eliminate a few academic specialties. It's one thing for someone to vote to eliminate the position of thirteenth-century Belgian economic philosophy and another thing entirely to vote to eliminate the job of Carrie or Tucker who always volunteers for institution-wide committees and is such a nice person to work with on them. Moreover, if Carrie or Tucker is rude, insolent, or virtually invisible on campus, someone may even be tempted to eliminate that position ahead of several others. In short, good relations with administrators is a smart career move, and many faculty members learn that lesson only when it's too late.

Nevertheless, this advice doesn't mean that all administrators are blameless and wonderful role models. In their survey of faculty members, the authors asked respondents whether they had ever reported to (either directly or indirectly through one or more administrative layers) an academic supervisor whom they regarded as dictatorial, rude to underlings, and/or unnecessarily authoritarian. Among those who took the survey, 58.8 percent said yes. They were then asked whether they had ever reported to (again either directly or indirectly through one or more administrative layers) an academic supervisor whom they regarded as immoral, unethical, and/or dishonest, and 29.4 percent said yes. The faculty members who participated in the survey were also asked whether they had ever regarded one of their direct or indirect supervisors as stupid, incompetent, and/or not up to the job intellectually. Almost half, 47 percent said yes. In other words, having a non-collegial or overly controlling boss is about twice as likely as having a corrupt boss, with the chance of having an unintelligent boss falling somewhere in between.

Those who took the survey were also asked to rank in importance the following attributes for college administrators:

- compassion
- enthusiasm
- perseverance
- creativity
- collegiality
- vision
- integrity
- a sense of humor
- courage
- passion for the job

Respondents ranked *integrity* as first in importance more than three times as often as the attribute that came in second: *collegiality*. Together those two qualities far exceeded all the rest in importance. In other words, most faculty members hope their administrators are going to be *supportive colleagues who act with integrity*. The rest of the attributes were given far less importance and were ranked in the following order: vision, passion for the job, compassion, creativity, courage, a sense of humor, perseverance, and enthusiasm. The authors gave the faculty members they contacted a chance to indicate which important administrative attributes were missing from the list of ten that on appeared the survey. The eight answers people provided most often were:

- empathy (by far the most common response)
- respect for others
- effective communication skills
- leadership
- political savvy
- a willingness to listen
- basic managerial skills
- support for diversity

Finally, the authors asked faculty members, if they could give just one piece of advice to administrators at all levels, what would it be? Some of the answers respondents provided were the following.

- Establish trust by supporting your staff.
- Don't assume the worst about people.
- Conduct important communication in person, and avoid believing that memos and email messages are effective substitutes for conversation.
- See your job as cultivating the people you supervise, not just enforcing policies or boosting productivity.
- Follow the Golden Rule.
- Be very careful with your language and professional ethics.
- Be respectful, diligent, and clear about what your needs and expectations are.
- Treat members of the faculty and staff as colleagues, even while you perform your supervisory tasks effectively.
- Always remember that your job is to listen and help improve those you supervise.
- Treat everyone with respect.
- Involve faculty members in every level of academic decision-making.
- Lead with compassion and get to know the knowledge of the skills of your staff.

CASE STUDY 4.2: DANGEROUS LIAISONS

Ever since you arrived at the university, you've had an excellent relationship with your chair, Dr. Casanova D'Amour. You've found him to be accessible, supportive, and always willing to offer a word of constructive advice. Recently, however, you've had reason to be concerned about the nature of the relationship that's developing between Dr. D'Amour and one of your graduate students, Jezebel Bovary.

Even though Jezebel's area of study isn't closely related to Dr. D'Amour's specialty, the two of them always seem to be together. They go to lunch off campus frequently and sit beside one another at the department's biweekly research symposium. A number of times you've gone to Dr. D'Amour's office to get his signature or to ask a quick question. While his door has almost always been open before, lately you find it closed each time. You knocked on the door during one visit and, when Dr. D'Amour opened the door slightly to ask what you wanted, you thought you caught a glimpse of Jezebel inside.

At a department meeting at which the topic of this year's graduate student awards came up, Dr. D'Amour eagerly nominated Jezebel for every single one. You've been impressed with Jezebel's work, but you know that the program also has many other excellent graduate students, a number of whom work directly with Dr. D'Amour. You find it strange that he seems so preoccupied with Jezebel, even though you can think of at least three or four other students more deserving of several of the awards.

Your institution has a strict policy forbidding romantic and/or sexual relationships between faculty members and students, even if those students are not in the faculty members' classes. The provost and director of human resources take this policy very seriously. You've known several tenured faculty members who were terminated for having had improper relationships with students, and you'd hate for Dr. D'Amour to suffer the same fate.

This term, one of your graduate classes meets from 6:00 to 9:00 p.m. on Thursdays. Jezebel's taking the class, and you've been wondering all semester whether you should speak to her, without making any accusations, about the importance of not letting relationships with members of the faculty develop in ways that could become problematic for them.

You've decided that tonight is the night you'll finally say something. But Jezebel gets out the door before you have a chance to stop her. You quickly gather up your materials and follow her to the parking lot. You get outside just in time to see a car pull up to the curb and Jezebel get inside. The driver is Dr. D'Amour.

Questions

1. Based only on what you know so far, what would you do?
2. What is likely to be the outcome for each of the following actions?
   a. You carry through with your plan to have an informal talk with Jezebel about appropriate and inappropriate faculty relationships.
   b. You tell Jezebel more directly about your concerns and mention that you saw her getting into Dr. D'Amour's car at night after class.
   c. You express your concerns to Dr. D'Amour, since you have a good, open relationship with him.
   d. You ask other students whether they suspect that anything improper is going on between Jezebel and Dr. D'Amour.
   e. You mention your concerns to the dean.
   f. You mention your concerns to the director of human resources.
   g. You mention your concerns to the campus's equal opportunity officer.
3. Would your response be any different if you knew that Dr. D'Amour were single?
   a. If you knew that Dr. D'Amour were married, would you openly express your concerns to his wife?
   b. If you knew that Dr. D'Amour were married, would you arrange for your concerns to reach his wife anonymously?
   c. If you knew that Dr. D'Amour were unhappily married, would your response be any different?
   d. If Dr. D'Amour and his wife often socialized with you and your significant other, would you handle the situation any differently?
4. Would your response be any different if you knew that one or more of the following were true?

a. If Dr. D'Amour had previously had an improper sexual relation-ship with a graduate student.
b. If Dr. D'Amour had previously been sanctioned for an im-proper sexual relationship with a graduate student and told, "This is your last chance."
c. If Jezebel Bovary had just come out of an abusive relationship.
d. If Jezebel Bovary always struck you as fragile, vulnerable, and easy to manipulate.
e. If Jezebel Bovary had a history of depression.
5. Would you change your answer if:
a. you were an untenured assistant professor?
b. you were a tenured full professor?
c. Dr. D'Amour were retiring in two years?
d. the institution had no policy against intimate faculty/student relationships?
e. the characters were named John Smith and Mary Jones instead of Casanova D'Amour and Jezebel Bovary?
f. Jezebel Bovary were the department chair, and Casanova D'Amour were the graduate student?

Resolution

You decide that, since Dr. D'Amour had always been supportive and accessible, you owed it to him to have a private conversation about your concerns. Alone with him in his office, with the door closed, you men-tion that the relationship he has with Jezebel Bovary conveys a percep-tion of possible impropriety, and you urge him to take steps to protect his career and Jezebel's future. You mention a few specific incidents when the relationship between the two of them seemed a bit too inti-mate and gave the appearance that the institution's policy on faculty/student relationships may be in danger of being violated.

Dr. D'Amour first seems shocked by what you're saying and then becomes angry. "There's absolutely nothing inappropriate going on between me and Jezebel Bovary," he thunders. "I just happen to think she's one of our best graduate students in years, and I'm surprised that you, as her advisor, would say such a thing. As for my giving her a ride after your class, she happened to mention that she was flying home that weekend to see her fiancé, and I offered her a ride to the airport since I live in that direction anyway. I find these accusations offensive, and I'm appalled that you would even think such a thing."

You try to calm Dr. D'Amour down by saying that you were merely trying to look out for his welfare and that, if the roles were reversed, you'd want him to be just as candid with you as you were with him. Your remarks help slightly, but the atmosphere is still frosty when you leave his office twenty minutes later.

A few weeks go by, and you do everything you can to improve your relationship with Dr. D'Amour. One day, however, another member of your department drops by your office and says, "Did you hear what happened to Dr. D'Amour? Apparently he's been having this big affair with Jezebel Bovary, and someone filed a complaint with the dean. Human Resources looked into it and found enough evidence to proceed. He's stepping down as chair immediately and may even lose his job over it."

As the conversation continues, you discover that Dr. D'Amour directly lied to you when you mentioned your concerns. Jezebel doesn't have a fiancé, the two of them had been in a romantic relationship for several months, and they went directly to a hotel after your class that night. Even worse, you learn that, in an effort to protect himself from your allegations, Dr. D'Amour had started spreading rumors about you and was trying to have your contract voided. That was what led another member of the department to file the complaint with the dean. You never discover who this anonymous benefactor was, but you feel very grateful for what he or she did.

CASE STUDY 4.3: A TALE OF TWO ADMINISTRATORS

Two of the administrators you report to couldn't be more different in character and leadership style. Your dean, Dr. Sunil ("Sunnie") Smiley, always appears to be in a good mood. He seems to genuinely care about students and faculty members in the college, attends campus events almost every night of the week, and never has a bad word to say about anyone. Your provost, however, Dr. Anna Bismal-Feyleur, is the complete opposite. Doctor Bismal-Feyleur has never been seen in a pleasant mood. She is a suspicious and mistrustful person. She sees any idea proposed by anyone other than herself as merely a plot to get out of doing any work. Her comments tend to be sarcastic, and more than one faculty member has been seen leaving her office on the verge of tears.

As part of Dr. Smiley's periodic evaluation, the provost surveyed every faculty member and department chair in the college to gain a sense of the dean's administrative effectiveness. She also is conducting a number of focus groups in which she'll talk with small groups of faculty members and administrators about their interactions with Dr. Smiley. Several years ago, when another dean was being evaluated, you suggested that the process be expanded to include staff members and students. The response you received was something that is known at your institution as "typical Bismal-Feyleur": Rather than taking your suggestion seriously, she mocked it and then turned her anger toward you for wasting her time with idiotic proposals. The exchange was so uncomfortable that you've gone out of your way to avoid Dr. Bismal-Feyleur ever since.

That strategy isn't possible now since the provost's office has "invited" you to be a member of one of the focus groups taking part in the dean's evaluation. You call the provost's secretary to offer some excuse about why you can't participate and are told, "Not attending the meeting isn't an option. When the provost issues an 'invitation,' it's a summons to appear, not a request." Grudgingly you go to the focus group where Dr. Bismal-Feyleur leads you and about a dozen other faculty members in what she promises will be a free and open discussion.

Within a few minutes, however, you realize that the discussion is anything but free and open. The provost simply ignores any positive comment about Dr. Smiley and zeroes in on even the slightest negative remark. "He arrived five minutes late at your department meeting?" she asked one participant. "How many other times did he cause problems for the college because of his deplorable time management skills?" Gradually, over the course of the meeting, you sense the mood of the other participants shifting against Dr. Smiley. The provost keeps using words like "weak," "ineffective," and "aimless" when speaking of the dean, and the others gradually pick up her vocabulary.

The whole process makes you very uncomfortable. You like Dr. Smiley and thinks he's been good for the college. You try several times to mention positive contributions the dean has made, but Dr. Bismal-Feyleur doesn't acknowledge your remarks. You make one last effort to come to Dr. Smiley's defense, and Dr. Bismal-Feyleur angrily shuts you down. "Will you stop getting us off track with this trivia? I'm trying to talk about important issues." You start to say that you thought you were called to this meeting because your views were important, but something in Dr. Bismal-Feyleur's withering look tells you that such a remark would be counterproductive.

After the meeting, you're walking across campus with several other participants, and you ask them why they started out so positive about Dr. Smiley but then "threw him under the bus" (in your words). "You could just see the handwriting on the wall," one of your colleagues says. "When the provost's out to get someone, that person's history. It became really clear that these focus groups are just an excuse to fire the dean. I mean Dr. Smiley's a nice guy and all, but I'm not going to risk my career for him."

You counter that you found the provost's approach manipulative and unprofessional. You regard Dr. Smiley's positive leadership style as refreshing and note that you can't understand why Dr. Bismal-Feyleur has to be so tough and bitter all the time. "I think we have to give her the benefit of the doubt," another faculty member says. "Remember how hard it must have been for her as a woman to reach such a high position here. I think she feels that, if she doesn't act tough and do everything she can to counter weakness, she'll appear to be weak herself."

Questions

1. Based solely on what you know so far:
    a. How do you respond to your colleagues?
    b. What, if anything, do you do with regard to Dr. Smiley?
2. What is likely to be the result if you took one of the following actions?
    a. You informed Dr. Smiley about what you saw at the focus group and learned from your faculty colleagues on your walk across campus.
    b. You made an appointment with Dr. Bismal-Feyleur to confront her with your belief that her actions have been manipulative and unprofessional.
    c. You expressed your concerns about Dr. Bismal-Feyleur to the president.

    d. You sent an anonymous note to the president about Dr. Bismal-Feyleur.

    e. You met with a local union representative to discuss your options.

    f. You began to organize the faculty in a "Save Dr. Smiley" movement.

    g. You shared your opinion with a member of the board of trustees whom you happen to know.

    h. You did nothing.

3. Would your response be any different if one or more of the following were true?

    a. If Dr. Smiley were intending to retire in two years.

    b. If you learned that Dr. Bismal-Feyleur did indeed have a difficult climb to her administrative position and had to overcome a great deal of sexism and opposition to achieve her status.

    c. If Dr. Bismal-Feyleur had a chronic condition that caused her constant pain.

    d. If there were reason to believe that Dr. Bismal-Feyleur's choice for the next dean of her college would be someone very much like herself.

    e. If Dr. Bismal-Feyleur were actively seeking the job of president of your university.

    f. If. Dr. Bismal-Feyleur were the institution's only female administrator.

4. Would you handle the situation any differently if Dr. Smiley were female and Dr. Bismal-Feyleur were male?

5. If you had to choose between the following alternatives, which would you prefer?

    a. The situation outlined in the case study: a congenial dean and an ill-tempered provost.

    b. The reverse of the situation outlined in the case study: an ill-tempered dean and a congenial provost.

    c. The same personalities but at a lower level in the hierarchy: a congenial department chair and an ill-tempered dean.

    d. The same personalities but at a higher level in the hierarchy: a congenial provost and an ill-tempered president.

Resolution

You begin by responding to your colleague's last remark. "Actually, I think it's rather sexist to assume that a woman might become a tough and bitter administrator just because she faced opposition along her career path. There are plenty of examples of women who became deans, provosts, and presidents with more positive, collegial styles of leadership. I think it sends the wrong message to try to excuse her because of her gender."

The discussion continues until you reach your office. You haven't been able to change anyone's mind, but you feel that you've done your best in making your point. However, the more you reflect on the situation, the more you believe that you can't just sit idly by while a good person is being poorly treated. Although Dr. Bismal-Feyleur may be acting without integrity, you conclude that there is no excuse for you not to adhere to high standards of decency and collegiality.

Because Dr. Smiley is so accessible, you feel that your first step should be to apprise him of what you believe is going on. Since you don't want to end-run your chair on such an important issue, you meet with the chair first, and the two of you go to speak to Dr. Smiley together. After you describe what has occurred, you realize that this is the first time you've ever seen the dean look sad and subdued. The dean wonders aloud whether he should just accept the inevitable and resign, but you and your chair urge him to hold on a little while longer before making such a drastic decision. You remind Dr. Smiley that he needs to think, not just of his own future, but also of the future of the entire college.

After further discussion with your chair, you discover that there are several more faculty members who are just as concerned about what the provost is doing as you are. You decide that it may be time to involve the president, even though you know the risks involved in such a move. As the old saying goes, "If you attack a king, you must kill the king": People in positions of power can be dangerous enemies if you try to undermine them but are not successful. You're particularly worried because the president and the provost have always seemed so close. The president speaks warmly about Dr. Bismal-Feyleur at public meetings and has noted, "We see eye-to-eye on most issues."

Despite these reservations, you keep to your principles and take the lead in expressing to the president your concerns about Dr. Bismal-Feyleur's integrity. She listens noncommittally through the entire meeting and, when everyone has had their say, simply thanks you all for trusting her enough to share these concerns. You leave thinking that, at best, you've wasted your time while, at worst, you may have created a situation that will turn the provost into a real enemy. You start wondering whether the time may be right to update your résumé.

Nearly a month later, however, the president's office sends a surprise announcement to the entire institutional community. It says that Dr. Bismal-Feyleur has announced her resignation as provost, effective immediately, and a search will soon be under way to find her replacement. In the meantime, Dr. Sunil Smiley will serve as interim provost. Rumors abound as to what occurred and why. You'd like to think that your meeting with the president played a role in this development, but you can't be sure. Several people claim to know from "reliable sources" that the president had been looking for a reason to get rid of the provost for a long time now. "I guess she couldn't stand her either," one of your friends says. "Apparently this integrity issue was just the last straw." Even though you never find out whether what you told the president led to the dismissal of Dr. Bismal-Feyleur, you're glad that you put principle ahead of your own career and did what you were convinced was the right thing to do.

BECOMING KNOWN FOR SOMETHING IMPORTANT

One highly effective way of establishing positive interactions with administrators is developing an area of professional responsibility that is valuable to the institution. This area of professional responsibility isn't the same as your academic specialty. That field is of critical importance, too, but this additional area of focus should be something related to the special needs of the college or university.

For example, every academic program needs someone who understands the intricacies of academic accreditation. Your regional accrediting association, which accredits the entire institution, may have procedures and requirements that are quite different from any type of special or professional accreditation that applies only to your academic field. Knowing these requirements and becoming a specialist in meeting them are efforts that serve the needs of the institution and increases your value in the eyes of the administration.

In addition to accreditation, there are plenty of other areas in which you could become the local expert: Assessment, grant writing, faculty development, budgeting, curriculum development, active learning strategies, online learning strategies, the state legislative process, interacting with the media, and countless other activities are all needed by the institution and offer you an opportunity to become known for something important. In fact, if you think it's at all possible that you'll serve as a department chair, dean, or head of the faculty senate someday, mastering one of these areas can be an important stepping-stone toward achieving your goal.

SCENARIO 4.1

You have a sincere interest in faculty development but are currently only in your second year on tenure-track.

Challenge Question:

Is now the right time to pursue faculty development as a special area of expertise?

Scenario Outcome:

You decide that the answer to this question depends on the meaning of the word *pursue*. It would not be wise to become heavily involved in conducting faculty development programs for the department, attending national conferences on faculty development, or chairing a very time-consuming committee in this area. While these activities would count as service, they're likely to consume time that you need right now in order to establish a strong record of teaching and research.

On the other hand, if pursuing this interest means either serving on a committee that doesn't detract from your other responsibilities or getting some advice from someone about the best ways to build your faculty development profile after you qualify for tenure, or both, then these activities can help lay a solid foundation for your eventual plans. You decide that you'll focus on teaching and research for now. But you'll pay special attention whenever issues of faculty development are raised at meetings and keep up with this topic by occasionally looking at websites devoted to programs of this sort.

SCENARIO 4.2

Although you want a full-time position, the best job you've been able to find is as a part-time instructor in your field.

Challenge Question:

Is it worthwhile to develop an area of professional expertise outside your discipline even though you won't be compensated for it?

Scenario Outcome:

You realize that not being compensated for this activity really means not being compensated *immediately and directly*. Even though the institution where you hold a part-time position won't pay you more for helping with their accreditation efforts or for assisting other faculty members with the development of online courses, engaging in these activities may help bring you to people's attention in a very positive way.

When a full-time position does become available, the school may look on you more favorably because you've already demonstrated that you're a good community citizen. And even if that school never has a full-time job in your field, your area of administrative expertise can be a good selling point when you apply for jobs elsewhere.

SCENARIO 4.3

You're a tenured full-professor who believes that retirement is about ten or fifteen years in the future.

Challenge Question:

Is it still useful to develop a new area of professional responsibility even though you've already established yourself in your career and have no more promotions ahead of you?

Scenario Outcome:

Finding a new area of professional responsibility has a great deal of value even for the most prestigious senior professors. First, it offers a way for them to give back to an institution that helped them achieve their professional goals. Second, it can bring new challenges and excitement on days when other academic responsibilities are beginning to seem routine. Third, even if your school does not yet have a procedure for post-tenure review, there's no guarantee that it won't develop one soon, and developing a new area of professional responsibility is a good way of demonstrating to administrators that you're still actively growing as a college professor.

FOR REFLECTION

Obviously, you're not the only one who's responsible for your positive interactions with administrators. It's up to the administrator, too, to want to have positive interactions with faculty members, regard them as important, and treat you and all your colleagues with respect. But you can go a long way toward improving even the tensest interactions with a chair, dean, provost, or president if you practice the Babel fish approach to communication that we explored in this chapter, demonstrate integrity and collegiality, and illustrate that you're a good institutional citizen by developing your own area of professional expertise and responsibility.

Not all administrators will be easy to work with, just as not all faculty members are collegial and dedicated to the interests of their students. But it's a good practice to give an administrator the benefit of the doubt, assume that he or she is seriously trying to do what's best for the institution, and adhere to the principles that you expect that administrator also to represent.

5

CONDUCTING RESEARCH SUCCESSFULLY

Research is integral to the work of being a college professor regardless of the institution where you work. At a community college where the teaching and service expectations are very high, research may consist largely of keeping up with changes that are occurring in one's field. At universities that have a designation of very high research activity in the Carnegie Classification of Institutions of Higher Education (i.e., the institutions that once were known as "Research 1 Universities"), expectations for peer-reviewed publications, external grants, patents, public exhibits or performances, and new discoveries will be significantly greater. But regardless of the type and amount of research our schools expect from us, one theme remains constant: One of the differences between a school teacher and a college professor can be found in the degree to which we expose our students to recently developed insights.

The amount and type of research we're expected to conduct varies with the type of institution we serve, and the form it takes varies with the discipline in which we work. For this reason, it's very important for college professors to know the expectations their institutions have for them in terms of the amount, variety, and format of the research they conduct. Research in chemistry looks very different from that in music. Research in marketing looks very different from that in engineering.

And research in education looks very different from that in architecture. So, it's important for college professors to know what the expectations of their own discipline and institution are in order to engage in the type of research that is appropriate to the positions they hold.

In the authors' survey of college professors, participants were asked how they felt about the amount of emphasis placed on research in American higher education in general when it comes to making personnel decisions about faculty members. Among the responses,

- 52.9 percent replied that the right amount of emphasis was placed on research,
- 23.5 percent said that research received far too much emphasis,
- 17.6 percent said that research received a bit too much emphasis, and
- 5.9 percent answered that too little emphasis was placed on research.

One respondent wrote, "Research tends to impede the performance of faculty in the classroom. Universities need to designate certain faculty as primarily teaching professors and designate other faculty as primarily research professors. Teaching suffers when faculty members find themselves in the publish-or-perish dilemma."

Another participant in the survey commented, "The way most institutions conduct faculty reviews is an easy way to outsource the legitimation of the faculty. Someone else's views as a peer reviewer replace our own efforts to get to know our faculty professionally, deeply observe and engage with their teaching, assess service and citizenship in meaningful ways, and so on. I would prefer more emphasis on annual work plans, asking each faculty member, 'Did you do what you said you'd do and we said we needed from you this year in the ongoing and organic life of this department?'" A third respondent stated, "Many of our institutions are teaching-focused but distort their personnel decisions by over-emphasizing published research because it's easier to quantify those results."

When participants in the survey were asked about the emphasis *their own institution* placed on research, the results became somewhat more bimodal. A larger percentage of respondents said they were satisfied with the weights their own school assigned the different aspects of faculty performance, but those who were not satisfied tended to be very dissatisfied. Although no one had replied that American higher education in general placed *far too little* emphasis on research, about one out of every eight respondents thought their own institution did. Among the survey responses,

- 62.5 percent replied that the right amount of emphasis was placed on research
- 18.7 percent said that research received a bit too much emphasis
- 12.5 percent answered that research received far too little emphasis
- 6.2 percent said that research received far too much emphasis

Here again the comments that college professors added to these responses were quite revealing. One faculty member wrote, "My school is a pretty good teaching university that's vainly trying to become a major (and greatly unneeded) research university. I feel we've lost our way." Another said, "At my university, we build in research expectations contingent upon the role of the faculty and the program. But most of our faculty do not do research in the strict sense of that term."

A third faculty member concluded, "Conducting research is, for many faculty members, an unfunded or underfunded mandate. For some units the productivity is legitimate: Grants are common, graduate students are available to assist, and other resources are in place. Yet it often seems that *all* units are then compared to that ideal." At the other end of the spectrum, one person wrote, "I do not believe my own institution places enough emphasis on traditional research. Although I have no problems using [Ernest] Boyer's ideas on the multiple forms that scholarship can take [as outlined in *Scholarship Reconsidered* (1997)], I think the university where I work allows too much to 'count' as scholarship."

Agreement was far broader when participants were asked, "Which do you think is the greater obstacle to faculty members in performing research: not enough funding or not enough time?" Responses divided as follows:

- 83.3 percent said not enough time
- 16.7 percent said not enough funding

A few observers put these results into context. One said, "At my university, faculty teach a 4-4 load and have heavy service commitments. I think they do not have sufficient time to conduct research." Another wrote, "Obviously it depends on the discipline. In my discipline conducting research is fairly inexpensive so the main obstacle is time. But the growing emphasis on applied learning (such as service learning) requires a great deal of effort and advance preparation by the faculty member. There are increased standards for assessment, legitimate service obligations, and other duties imposed on the faculty. In such a system, research is bound to be slighted."

The survey asked participants to what extent they thought good teaching correlated with good research. Among the responses,

- 45.5 percent answered that there was some degree of correlation
- 27.3 percent said there was only a very small correlation
- 18.2 percent believed there was a strong correlation
- 9.1 percent concluded that there was no discernible correlation

One of the respondents added, "Good writing and organizing of arguments promotes a better awareness of audience, clarity of presentation, and organizational habits that translate into better teaching in the classroom. Being aware of the literature also helps faculty members incorporate relevant examples or consider opinions/arguments that do not necessarily agree with their own positions on issues. It also enables faculty members to guide students in their own thinking on issues of relevance to the course." But not everyone was convinced. Another respondent wrote, "Teaching and research have an almost negative correlation. For most faculty members, the more time you spend conducting your own research, the less time you spend mastering your pedagogical techniques. It's as simple as that."

CASE STUDY 5.1: YOU MEAN YOU CALL *THIS* RESEARCH?

You are appointed to a personnel committee that is charged with evaluating the performance of faculty members from across the institution.

For each of the following faculty members that you're asked to review, decide whether the scholarly activity he or she conducted over the past year would be considered appropriate in both quality and quantity for a faculty member in that rank and discipline at your institution. If your institution doesn't happen to offer the discipline indicated, imagine that it did and base your conclusion on your sense of what would be appropriate in the closest possible fields that *are* represented at your school.

- **Professor A** is an assistant professor of family and consumer sciences (the study of effective ways of managing the home, including nutrition, child development, and hygiene) who has spent the past year developing, but not yet conducting, an online survey that will determine the vitamin content of the average evening meal of middle-class families in the Los Angeles metropolitan area.
- **Professor B** is an associate professor of accounting (the theory and system of creating, maintaining, and auditing the financial records of a person or entity) who this year, as part of a paid consultancy, developed a new type of cloud-based financial records system for a start-up company.
- **Professor C** is a full professor of sport and exercise science (the application of scientific principles and techniques with the aim of improving athletic performance) who developed a radically new training regime that reduces soccer injuries by 11 percent.
- **Professor D** is an associate professor of nursing (the preparation of professionals in the field of health care who will work to achieve improved health outcomes for individuals, families, and communities) who during the past year has written several policy papers designed to streamline nursing practices at local hospitals.
- **Professor E** is a full professor of marine biology (the scientific study of organisms living in or depending on the oceans) who spent the past year studying the diet of invasive lionfish off the Outer Banks of North Carolina.
- **Professor F** is an assistant professor of dance (the art of rhythmic movement usually performed with musical accompaniment) who spent most of the current academic year preparing for and staging a modern adaptation of *Coppélia* with a cast of non-professionals at a local community theater.

You're given no information that allows you to judge the quality of the research. Assume that, in each case, when you ask someone you trust in that discipline if the research in question was of suitable quality, the answer you received was, "Oh, yes. I took a look at that, and I personally thought it was pretty good."

Questions

1. Based only on what you know so far, which activities would probably not be considered appropriate in both quality and quantity for a faculty member in that rank and discipline at your institution?
2. Would your answer be any different if one or more of the following were true?
   a. If the faculty member received a two-course release from teaching each semester during the past year to conduct this research
   b. If the faculty member presented this work at a state conference in his or her discipline
   c. If the faculty member presented this work at a national conference in his or her discipline
   d. If the faculty member published an article about this work in a trade journal commonly purchased at local drugstores
   e. If the faculty member published an article about this work in a peer-reviewed journal from a university press
   f. If a scholar in this same discipline at a state college not far from you wrote a letter indicating that this work met the standards of college-level research in that field
   g. If a scholar in this same discipline at Harvard University wrote a letter indicating that this work met the standards of college-level research in that field
3. If your answer changed on the basis of any of the additional information in question #2 above, what general principles can you derive about what constitutes legitimate research at your institution?

Resolution

Since you were instructed to base your answers on expectations at your own institution, it's not possible to draw conclusions that will apply to every college or university. Nevertheless, as you reflect on your own views about what constitutes appropriate forms of research at your school, consider the degree to which the following factors played a part in your decision.

- The quantity of the research
- The time investment required by the research
- The way in which results of the research were disseminated
- Whether the appropriateness of the research was validated by professionals outside your own discipline
- Whether the results were reproducible
- Whether the project had logical consistency (i.e., it seemed to make sense)
- Whether the results were free from bias

Ask yourself, too, whether your own standards of appropriate forms and levels of research seem to differ in any way from those expected at your institution. If you do note a difference, what might account for this disparity?

CASE STUDY 5.2: CHANGING RESEARCH FOCUS

You're a full professor who has served your institution faithfully for twenty-one years. Your chair trusts your opinion in the area of research because you have so many successful grants, peer-reviewed publications, and patents to your name. One of your proudest accomplishments is having served as a mentor to four current members of your department, all of whom are now productive researchers. Their tenure and promotion applications sailed through the various committees at the institution, and each of these colleagues still stops by your office to ask for advice on a regular basis.

One day, during a casual conversation with your chair, you happen to mention how proud you are of everything these protégés have done. "Yes, well," you chair begins hesitantly, "it's really the mentoring you've done for others that made me want to talk to you today." Your ears perk up at this turn in the discussion. "I think our most recent hire, Professor Rebel Yell, could use a little mentoring, and I think you're just the person to do it."

Your spirits sink at this news. You know all about the problems caused by Professor Rebel Yell. Members of the department were all pleased throughout the interview process four years ago because Professor Yell came across as confident, self-assured, and full of fresh ideas. Since joining the faculty, however, those same traits have increasingly caused difficulties for the young professor. Professor Yell has assumed a role of sticking up for the underdog and aggressively challenging anyone viewed as a figure of authority. Everyone who's an administrator at the university has been on the receiving end of one of Professor Yell's tirades about injustice and insensitivity to the needs of the faculty. As a well-established senior faculty member, you also know what it's like to be the target of Professor Yell's ire.

While this behavior has created a strain in interpersonal relations, student evaluations of Professor Yell's courses are always very positive. You've been impressed by the preparation of students who have taken Professor Yell's classes. But Professor Yell uses this success as a bludgeon against other faculty members who, in the professor's own opinion, aren't doing everything they can to help the students. Faculty assemblies and committee meetings can be painful whenever Professor Yell is present. The standard argument is that no one else is changing fast enough to suit the changing nature of your discipline. The entire curriculum needs to be rewritten from top to bottom. People's teaching techniques are too old-fashioned. (Some professors are even still requiring students to attend class, a practice that Professor Yell regards as utterly archaic.) And every faculty member's research needs to be redirected from the stale topics of the past to emerging issues in the discipline.

Professor Yell doesn't merely give lip service to these ideas. Over the past three years, Professor Yell's research has gradually moved into an area far different from the specialty for which this faculty member was hired. That research has been successful in its own terms—Professor Yell now has seven peer-reviewed articles in good journals and a grant proposal that will probably receive significant external funding—but the type of research the program hoped the new faculty member would do hasn't developed at all. It's the nature of the research that the chair wants to discuss with you today.

"I can't imagine the department, much less the university-wide committee, making a positive recommendation for tenure and promotion if this trendy, rather shallow 'research' continues," your chair says. "This area that Professor Yell is working in is just a fad, and no one's going to care about it in a few years. But I do believe there's enough time to turn this situation around. What Professor Yell needs is some good, mature guidance. And you're just the person to provide it. See if you can get Professor Yell back on track."

You can already predict what would happen if you did what the chair asked. Every conversation with Professor Yell would result in an argument, and you'd be accused of standing in the way of progress. Inevitably the tenure and promotion process would be a battle. The chair is probably right: It will be difficult getting a positive vote at several stages in the process, and that means a prolonged and bitter appeal, grievance procedure, and lawsuit. But by appearing to try to stifle Professor Yell's academic freedom, you could just be moving that battle up a few years. The whole affair is beginning to look like a no-win situation.

Questions

1. What is likely to be the outcome if you chose the following responses?
    a. You tell the chair that you'll think about it and then simply ignore the request. You hope that the chair will forget about the issue, take the hint, or ask someone else.
    b. You tell the chair that you'll mentor Professor Yell.
    c. You tell the chair that you don't think it's a good idea for you to mentor Professor Yell.
    d. You tell the chair that you'll have a conversation with Professor Yell and mention these concerns, but you won't serve as a formal mentor.
    e. You recommend that, instead of you, one of the faculty members you mentored previously now "pay it forward" by mentoring Professor Yell.
    f. You recommend that the senior members of the program mentor Professor Yell collectively.

   g. You recommend that a mixed group of newer and more established faculty members in the discipline mentor Professor Yell
collectively.

   h. You recommend that, instead of singling out Professor Yell,
the department discuss at a faculty meeting the risks involved
in moving away from the research specialty you were hired in.

2. Would your response be any different if one or more of the following were true?

   a. If Professor Yell were further along in the probationary period
and were going to be reviewed for tenure and promotion next
year

   b. If Professor Yell came to you personally and requested you to
act as a mentor

   c. If Professor Yell did not have good teaching evaluations and a
history of solid peer-reviewed research

   d. If Professor Yell were a member of a severely underrepre-
sented ethnic group at your university

   e. If Professor Yell were the opposite gender from what you assumed as you read this case study

3. How much academic freedom and authority should faculty members have over the focus of their own research agenda? Where does
the line get drawn between a college professor's right to explore
innovative, new specialties and the institution's right to have a professor work within the specialty he or she was hired for?

Resolution

You tell your chair that, although you're quite willing to help Professor Yell, you don't think it's a good idea for you to work as a formal mentor in this case. You outline your reasons why you believe the strategy
the chair has proposed is ill-advised.

- It's in the nature of academic disciplines to grow, change, and try
out new ideas. While Professor Yell may have created some interpersonal challenges by the aggressive way in which other people's
teaching and research has been challenged, there's no denying
that Professor Yell's record of teaching and publication has been

successful. You believe it would be wrong to try to redirect the research agenda of a highly productive faculty member.

- While you're sensitive to the need of the department to have its faculty members perform the duties they were hired to do, you're less concerned than your chair about how this issue relates to research. You say, "As long as Professor Yell is still teaching the courses we need to have covered, I think we can afford to be a little flexible about a shift in research focus. Just as disciplines grow, change, and try out new ideas, so do we have an obligation to let our faculty members grow, change, and try out new ideas. I think we should be encouraging Professor Yell to explore these new paths, and not get in the way."

- Professor Yell has demonstrated hostility to authority figures, including yourself, who are perceived as standing in the way of progress. You consider it unlikely that this faculty member would be receptive to any suggestions coming from you, no matter how well-intentioned those suggestions may be.

- You suggest that a more appropriate role for you might be to serve as an advocate for the significance and quality of Professor Yell's research when the promotion and tenure process occurs. You can do so in good conscience on the basis of Professor Yell's publication record, grant proposal, and success in incorporating current research into coursework. An added advantage of this approach would be that it suggests to Professor Yell that not all of the senior faculty and administration are opposed to new ideas and the evolution of the discipline.

The chair leaves the conversation unpersuaded by your thoughts and continues to suggest to other senior faculty members that they mentor Professor Yell. You don't know exactly how the word gets out, but one day Professor Yell stops by your office and says, "I hear you stood up for me and my research with our chair."

You minimize your role by saying that you just believe disciplines change over time and there's a need for academics to approach new ideas with an open mind. Professor Yell thanks you for saying so and asks your advice about how to get through to your colleagues in the department. "Give them time," you say, "and we'll bring them around." In the meantime, you suggest that Professor Yell might want to present some current research at a department forum and recommend submitting an article to one of the more traditional journals in your discipline that you know others on the faculty respect.

Periodically thereafter you meet with Professor Yell to discuss research and strategies for introducing new ideas to others in an effective manner. Neither of you ever uses the word *mentor* but, in your heart of hearts, you know that you're now mentoring your fifth colleague in the program and that this faculty member has a bright future ahead.

DEVELOPING A RESEARCH AGENDA

Everyone who conducts research has an agenda, even if they don't articulate it in words. An informal research agenda might consist of a general notion of the questions that interest the college professor, a flexible timetable for addressing those questions, and some basic ideas about how the answers to those questions will be shared with others. A more formal research agenda would be a written statement that specifies the faculty member's scholarly interests and priorities, a rationale for those priorities, an outline of the resources (time, money, facilities, labor, and equipment) that would be required to conduct the research, and a calendar for when various milestones and achievements should be anticipated.

Institutions and the programs within those institutions also have research agendas. By deciding to focus on scholarly activity in certain areas, the institution is better able to leverage its resources in a way that makes the most effective use of limited resources. It's always disappointing to be a faculty member whose area of interest doesn't appear to be reflected in the research priorities of his or her institution. Nevertheless, increasingly detailed institutional research agendas are becoming common as schools seek to fulfill ambitious missions of teaching and discovery while budgets decrease and opposition to high tuition rates grows.

The challenge for college professors is to find ways of aligning their own personal research agendas with those of their institutions. At times, this alignment requires use of the Babel fish approach to communication that we explored in chapter 4: Describing what you want to do by using language and concepts that are meaningful to the person hearing them. In other words, if your field of expertise is organizational theory, and your institution has decided to build research pillars of excellence in neuroscience, nanotechnology, and bioinformatics, you have two options. You can either try to argue that organizational theory is simply a more important field than those selected by the university (a strategy that is likely to fail), or you can describe your research as a means of supporting, reinforcing, or advancing work in such areas as neuroscience, nanotechnology, and bioinformatics.

Even if your school has not yet developed a detailed research agenda, there are advantages in having your own. It helps you clarify the impact of what you hope to accomplish to those who will be funding that research. It enables you to see broader connections between your teaching and research roles. And it gives you a more specific timetable for your work that you can share with your supervisor to see if he or she concurs with your plan.

SCENARIO 5.1

A professor of medieval literature believes that his or her discipline is being undervalued by an institution that has been investing more heavily in STEM disciplines (science, technology, engineering, and mathematics) and professional fields like business, nursing, and architecture. As a result, the professor is frequently unsuccessful when applying for internal research funding. In addition, the professor is the author of several well-reviewed books published by major university presses but has never been the recipient of an institutional award for excellence in research.

Challenge Question:

What should the professor do?

Scenario Outcome:

The faculty member in this scenario perceives a growing disparity between the research agenda of the institution and his or her own personal research agenda. There are several possible ways of responding. The college professor could conclude that the difference between his or her own priorities and those of the institution have become too great to bridge, and begin applying for positions at schools with a stronger dedication to the liberal arts. The professor could simply accept his or her identity as a member of a "service discipline" that will never play a leading role in the research mission of the institution. The professor could fight aggressively on behalf of the liberal arts and humanities, arguing that they are currently undervalued and need to be given a position of prominence at the institution. Or the professor could find a way of demonstrating that the study of medieval literature promotes critical thinking and other skills that have values for students in all fields and that research in this area should thus be recognized as significant.

The professor considers these options and decides that there are still many reasons for staying at the institution: The students are wonderful, the area is pleasant, and he or she has made many friends there. As a result, the professor will work through the four options listed above in reverse order. He or she will begin by demonstrating the valuable role that the liberal arts and humanities play in any academic program and by arguing that the school needs to give these disciplines greater funding and attention. Accepting a service role and considering a switch to another institution will be saved as last resorts.

SCENARIO 5.2

Your chair has asked to meet individually with each member of the department to discuss his or her research agenda for the next five years. In preparation for this meeting, you have drafted a document that outlines two primary focal points for your ongoing research and connects those areas to the institution's strategic plan, summarized a list of articles on these topics you expect to submit for publication, specified the journals that you hope will accept those articles, identified two possible grant opportunities to secure additional funding, and prepared a timetable for when you expect to reach these various milestones.

One of your colleagues shares with you the document that he or she is planning to bring to the meeting with the chair. It is a sparse, widely spaced set of bullet points that doesn't even begin to cover a single page. All that your colleague has written is the following:

- Try to write at least one article a year.
- Apply for a grant.
- Mentor graduate students.

When you express your surprise at your colleague's lack of specificity, the answer you receive is, "Look, it's a meaningless exercise anyway. No one's ever going to do exactly what they write down on a piece of paper. Life happens. New opportunities arise. My statement may look a little weird, but it's the most honest research agenda our chair's going to get. I'm not going to give the chair ammunition to use against me if I don't meet some specific goal that I set."

Challenge Questions:

How do you respond? Did you err on the side of being too specific or did your colleague err on the side of being too general?

Scenario Outcome:

As you think about it, both you and your colleague have a point. After all, it's useful to plan, but highly detailed plans never work out exactly as you expect. Nevertheless, having a research agenda as detailed as yours gives you some goals to work toward and helps crystallize your ideas as you move forward. Most chairs and deans understand that research agendas are unlikely to be fulfilled precisely as written. But they do help with planning and can be instrumental in helping you attain research funding. You decide to keep your statement as specific as it is, but just to be on the safe side, you add a sentence noting that changes to this agenda will necessarily occur as new opportunities arise and circumstances change.

ADVICE TO FACULTY MEMBERS ON RESEARCH

In their survey, the authors asked college professors what they would say if they could give one piece of advice about research to a brand-new, untenured faculty member. Among the answers given by respondents were the following:

- Teach at a community college if you just want to teach, but don't teach in certain regions of the country unless you want a low salary. The pay tells faculty how much education is valued in those regions.
- Put your students first by being great in the classroom. *Then* worry about your research.
- There will be many different forces at work that attempt to pull you away from your scholarship. Certainly, your teaching will demand much time from you. But so will your life outside of work, which you must not neglect. If you add into that equation the many demands placed on college professors to serve their institutions and their disciplines, you can easily be pulled away from investing time and effort into your scholarship. But you must resist. Spend fifteen to thirty minutes per day engaged in scholarship, whether it is writing a page or two of a paper, reading half a journal article, or reading half a chapter of a book relevant to your research project. Treat it as a class meeting. And jealously guard it against everything else.
- Synergize your efforts. Use lecture examples as the basis of conference papers and then use conference papers as the basis of publications.
- Make research a central focus. It may not be very important, but that's how the game is played.

That advice differed substantially from what people would tell an associate professor who was struggling to get promoted to the rank of full professor. Among the suggestions respondents made in this situation were these:

- Examine carefully the reasons why you want to be promoted to full professor. Is it simply for the salary increase? If so (and if research is not your greatest strength), there may be easier and more satisfying ways of increasing your income than trying to do something you're not cut out to do.
- Talk to the professor who is most successful at receiving funding. Ask that person to become your mentor.
- Prioritize your service to the institution and make that the hallmark of your career.

- Write one page of material per week. I know all too well the demands that university life and personal life place on associate professors. I was one for a *very* long time. But when I committed to writing one page per week, I suddenly found myself cranking out the same number of manuscripts for publication and for conference submission that I did when I first started as an assistant professor and had much more time and energy. Now, however, I found that I was thinking much more maturely about what I wrote and received much more satisfaction from writing it.
- Feel free to reinvent yourself and modify or even change your focus. Figure out a way to regard this transformation as a natural evolution, an extension and illustration of the same lifelong learning we want our students to model.

CASE STUDY 5.3: WHEN THE GROUND MOVES UNDER YOU

As a tenured faculty member and master teacher, you've seen many changes in the past few years as a faculty member in the School of Hard Knocks at Severely Underfunded State University (SUSU). A new president arrived three years ago, and she has replaced many administrators and embarked on a new strategic plan that emphasizes research. The provost hired by the president shares this vision, as does your dean who arrived only this year from a highly selective private university that is distinguished for its large endowment and the quality of its research.

The strategy the new administration is using to build SUSU's research portfolio is based on a performance-funding model. Each program has been assigned an aggressive new set of Key Performance Indicators (KPIs), all of which focus on peer-reviewed research in top-tier journals, scholarly books (but not textbooks) from a specified list of major university presses, large research grants, and international awards. The KPIs were set without input from the faculty, and they have been the subject of much friction between the faculty and administration ever since.

Departments that score well on the new KPIs will have their budgets increased, and their faculty will be eligible for a new pool of merit salary increases. Those that do moderately well will be left unchanged. The lowest 10 percent of the programs will have their budgets reduced and may even be phased out. In this way, the highly productive research programs can be rewarded without an increase in the institution's overall budget.

The result, as many members of the faculty see it, is that the rich will get richer while the poor get poorer. Programs that are already well funded for research will be able to make the transition to the new KPIs without much difficulty. Programs that are small and inadequately funded, unsupported by large federal grants due to the nature of their disciplines, or focused more on teaching than research will be penalized. The School of Hard Knocks definitely falls into this latter category.

You are worried about the impact the administration's new strategy will have on your program and, by extension, your own job. In the past SUSU was known as a great teaching university with a very strong service component. As a result, faculty members tended to be hired, tenured, and promoted to the rank of full professor largely based on the quality of their teaching. In your own program, a faculty member who produced an article every two or three years was considered to be active in scholarship. Under the new guidelines, even an article a year might not pass muster if it wasn't published by the "right" journal.

During your annual performance evaluation, your chair notes the mandate that's been passed down by the president. Although your teaching has been good, and your service has been commendable, the chair says you'll need to "step it up considerably" in terms of your research. When you ask precisely what the chair means, you're told that you'll need to more than double your annual rate of articles during the coming year, have them accepted by more prestigious journals, and apply for an external grant of at least a million dollars.

You reply that you don't have any idea how to find an agency that would fund a grant that large in your discipline; your chair counters by giving you the name of a grant facilitator in the office of research. You continue that you've been publishing as much as you believe you can and that these new standards are unreasonable; the chair refers ominously to a new post-tenure review policy that the provost will implement next year. That policy, the chair says, is aimed at "getting rid of the deadwood" and makes it clear how seriously the university will take its new emphasis on research.

Your chair then changes tactics and tries to give you a rousing pep talk about how you can achieve these new goals and reinvent yourself. Despite the chair's best efforts, however, you leave the meeting feeling like one of James Bond's martinis: shaken but not stirred.

Questions

1. What is likely to be the result if you took one of the following actions?
   a. You did nothing, planning to wait out the current administration with the expectation that a new president, provost, and dean would probably be arriving in about five years with new strategic goals that would render the current plan obsolete.
   b. You tried to organize the faculty of the School of Hard Knocks into a unified resistance against the new performance metrics.
   c. You met with representatives of the faculty union to discuss what options they could suggest for having the new research expectations scaled back.
   d. You made an effort to meet the new research expectations, submitted a grant proposal (that ended up not being funded), and slightly increased, but did not double, your production of refereed articles.
2. Would your decision be any different if one of the following were true?
   a. If you were an associate professor who still wanted to be promoted to the rank of professor
   b. If there was a realistic chance that the entire School of Hard Knocks would be phased out should the new KPIs not be met
   c. If the president had changed institutions after only three years at each of her last four jobs
   d. If you intended to retire in three years
   e. If, unlike the situation described in the scenario, you were untenured
   f. If, unlike the situation described in the scenario, you could count on the chair to advocate on your behalf

Resolution

Your experience at Severely Underfunded State University causes you to draw two important conclusions. First, you feel that the new strategic direction of the institution is too extreme a departure from what made it great in the past. You believe that the president wants to take credit for making SUSU a major research university, even though its reputation was built on the quality of its teaching and there's not the right infrastructure to support the president's goal. Second, you're aware that new administrations do like to be seen as acting decisively, and cutting programs they regard as unproductive is a common way for them to appear decisive.

As a result, you decide to proceed with a multipronged strategy. You'll "step it up" in research, as your chair requests, but not at the expense of your teaching, which has been the source of past success both for you and the institution as a whole. You don't yet have enough evidence to know whether this new emphasis on research is just a fad or a genuine trend, so you assume your wisest choice is to hedge your bets.

At the same time, you'll collect data on the value that the School of Hard Knocks provides to Severely Underfunded State University by indicating how much tuition revenue would be lost if the institution no longer offered those majors, how many programs would decline in quality because they lost access to the service courses that the school provides, and how much of the endowment would have to be returned to donors who gave restricted gifts to the school. With these strategies in place, you believe that you can keep your career and program safe at least until you can determine how lasting the use of the new KPIs will be and whether the next president's strategic plan bears any resemblance to that developed by the current president.

RESEARCH INTEGRITY

In the wake of widespread condemnation of the use of prisoners for medical experiments during the Second World War—as well as the Tuskegee Syphilis Experiment, in which African Americans living in Alabama were allowed to go untreated after developing syphilis; the Stanford Prison Experiment, in which students who were randomly selected to be "guards" began to impose sadistic penalties on students who were randomly selected to be "prisoners"; and similar events—the National Commission for the Protection of Human Subjects of Biomedical and Behavioral Research was established to develop policies preventing further mistreatment of human subjects. In the late 1970s, that commission released what has come to be known as the Belmont Report, a policy that bases standards for the treatment of human subjects based on three principles:

1. **Respect for persons:** Human beings must be treated with dignity and properly informed of any risks associated with an experiment for which they volunteer. Those whose capacity to make their own decisions is diminished due to age or illness should be accorded an even higher level of protection.
2. **Beneficence.** There should be an attempt to minimize harm and maximize benefits whenever human subjects are involved in an experiment.
3. **Justice.** The subjects of research should not be unduly disadvantaged because of their status (for example, experiments should not be conducted on prisoners because they are, quite literally, a captive audience) or deprived of benefits because of their poverty (for example, therapies developed through testing on human subjects should not be priced in such a way as to make the cost prohibitive for all but the very wealthy).

As an outgrowth of the Belmont Report, colleges and universities appoint an Institutional Review Board (IRB) that examines the protocol proposed for each experiment on human subjects that it to be conducted by any member of that institution. The goal of this review is to determine whether the investigators are taking appropriate measures to protect the participants. In a similar way, institutions are required to have an Institutional Animal Care and Use Committee (IACUC) that reviews protocols for experiments involving animals to determine that procedures are in place to avoid unnecessary suffering.

Research integrity involves far more than respecting the rights of people and animals, however. It also requires scholars to report their findings accurately, cite contributions made by others, and provide researchers with sufficient information to reproduce their results if necessary. Generally accepted research protocols are to be used to protect the safety of the public and the reliability of the results. For example in laboratory experiments, chemicals must be handled and stored correctly, protective clothing and eyewear must be worn, potentially harmful fumes must be vented properly, and so on. Whenever appropriate, the researcher's *conceptual framework*—the body of theories and assumptions within which he or she is operating—should be disclosed so that observers will understand the basic assumptions upon which the scholar's conclusions have been based.

CASE STUDY 5.4: DO THE DATA ADD UP?

In addition to your teaching duties, you supervise a research and development laboratory that is an important part of your institution's strategic plan. For the past two years you've really enjoyed your work because one of the tenured associate professors in your department, Dr. Dubious, has been serving in your lab as Principal Investigator (PI) on a five-year multi-million-dollar grant from a federal agency. As such, Dr. Dubious oversees the day-to-day operation of the project, has ultimate responsibility for collecting, analyzing, interpreting, and disseminating all the data related to the grant project, and is currently preparing the Continuing Grant Application that will ensure funding of the project for the next fiscal year.

You co-wrote the grant application with Dr. Dubious and serve as its project director, hiring staff as needed, submitting reports to the federal agency on a regular basis, verifying that the money is being appropriated to the correct object class category of the grant, and performing similar duties. When Dr. Dubious completes the Continuing Grant Application, you sign it and submit it to the federal agency. After it is reviewed, you're informed that you've received full funding for the third year of the grant, as you fully expected you would.

Your assistant project director on the grant, Skittish P. Whistleblower, is currently in a doctoral program in your department. You know Skittish particularly well from several classes that you taught and from your work as one of the advisors on Skittish's dissertation. As a result, you're not surprised when Skittish asks you to lunch one day, but you are surprised by what you learn there.

"I really don't know what to do," Skittish tells you. "As you know, part of the data we're collecting involves this huge survey that took so long to get approved by the IRB. The other day when I was returning some files to the lab, I saw Dr. Dubious change some of the responses on the forms we received from Disagree to Strongly Agree. I didn't feel I could say anything at the time. But I waited around and, at the end of the day, I found a large number of completed survey forms in the garbage that had been shredded. It looks to me as though Dr. Dubious replaced those forms with fabricated data and destroyed the forms we actually received from the participants."

You ask whether Skittish had kept the shredded survey forms. "No, I was too upset and confused. I guess I wasn't thinking straight. Now I'm afraid that, if Dr. Dubious learns I have these suspicions, my whole PhD program will be in jeopardy. I can't afford my advisor to distrust me or, worse, retaliate in some way and just cover up how the data were manipulated."

You try to calm Skittish down the best you can, but you have your own reason to be nervous. You had just sent in the Continuing Grant application, affirming that all proper protocols had been followed, with your signature on it. If you do nothing and it turns out that the integrity of the project was violated, your own reputation will be at stake. But if you confront Dr. Dubious and there's a reasonable explanation for what Skittish Whistleblower witnessed, you'll have damaged your relationship with a close colleague in way that might be irreparable.

Questions

1. What is likely to be the result if you took one of the following actions?
   a. You did nothing immediately but decided to keep a close eye on Dr. Dubious's collection and reporting of data to see whether any discrepancies or questionable practices occur in the future.
   b. You contact your federal agency and discuss your concerns about the possibility that data were fabricated in this study.
   c. You contact the human resources office at your institution.

d. You meet with your institution's research office to discuss the implications that would occur if the allegations are proven.

e. You contact your chair or dean to discuss this matter.

f. You hold a meeting with Dr. Dubious to discuss the allegations you've heard without bringing up Skittish's name.

g. You hold a meeting with Dr. Dubious to discuss the allegations you've heard and reveal the source of those charges.

h. You hold a meeting with all members of the grant project team to discuss the possibility that some of the data have been fabricated.

i. You ask Dr. Dubious to produce the responses to the survey instrument.

j. You conduct your own fact-finding mission by interviewing all people who might also have witnessed Dr. Dubious changing survey responses.

k. You conduct your own fact-finding mission by interviewing some of the respondents to the survey in order to determine whether their recollection of their responses tallies with the data that Dr. Dubious recorded.

2. Would your decision be any different if any of the following were true?

a. If your research laboratory were highly dependent for its continuation on the indirect cost recovery from this grant

b. If Dr. Dubious were not a tenured associate professor, as indicated in the case study, but an untenured assistant professor

c. If Dr. Dubious were not the dissertation advisor for Skittish Whistleblower

d. If this matter involved only an internally funded institutional grant, not an externally funded federal grant

e. If Skittish Whistleblower had retained the shredded survey forms

f. If you knew that Dr. Dubious and Skittish Whistleblower had clashed repeatedly over Skittish's dissertation and there was a long history of charges and countercharges between them.

3. Do you believe that the names assigned to the characters in this case study, Dr. Dubious and Skittish P. Whistleblower, may have preconditioned you to make certain assumptions about what occurred?

Resolution

After a sleepless night, you decide that ethical standards should never be compromised because challenging them would cause an unpleasant encounter, loss of face, or a financial loss. As a research professional, you have a responsibility to delve aggressively but fairly into this allegation of impropriety. Moreover, as project director, you have a fiduciary responsibility to do so as well. You decide that you have to look into the suspicions that were brought to you. You'll try to keep Skittish's name out of the matter for as long as you can, but you know that you can't guarantee anonymity in so serious a matter.

You decide that the first conversation you should have is with the research office at your institution. The result of that discussion is that there's sufficient reason to investigate the matter further, and so you and the vice president for research sit down with Dr. Dubious and discuss the allegations that have been made.

"I'm surprised at you," Dr. Dubious says to you at the meeting after you've summarized what you heard. "You of all people should have known precisely why I shredded those forms. One of the agreements we made with the IRB was that, due to the highly confidential nature of what people were disclosing in the survey, anyone who requested it by checking a box on the form could have the document shredded immediately after the data were recorded. In that way, the likelihood that anyone would recognize a respondent's handwriting and use the information inappropriately would be reduced. Shedding those forms didn't violate our protocol; it *was* our protocol."

"That may be," the vice president for research replies, "but what about the witness who saw you changing answers on some of the survey forms?"

"I wasn't *changing* answers," Dr. Dubious responds with exasperation. "I was *darkening* existing answers. Our scanner doesn't pick up marks that are blurred or too light. Particularly if people change their own answers from, say, Disagree to Strongly Agree, our scanner can get confused and register the mistaken response. So, on forms where someone tried to erase an answer, I merely erased it better and darkened the answer they really wanted. Once again, I was trying to *protect* the integrity of the data. Who told you all this anyway? Was it Skittish P. Whistleblower?"

"We're not going to disclose our source," the vice president for research interjects. "But from now on, I'm going to require that, if you
shred any more survey forms or 'darken' any more survey responses,
you do so in collaboration with your project director or assistant project
director so that there's no doubt in anyone's mind as to what's going on.
For now, though, I'm going to close the file on these allegations."

Not coincidentally, you're asked to take over as the major advisor on
Skittish P. Whisteblower's dissertation a few weeks later. Doctor Dubious and Skittish continue to work together on the grant and, although
their personal relationship becomes somewhat frosty, they both work
diligently to put the past behind them and complete the project in a
professional manner.

FOR REFLECTION

Teaching, research, and service often feel as though they are pulling
college professors in three separate directions. As much as possible,
therefore, it's important to find ways of bringing these three activities
together.

- Which aspects of your current research could enhance your teaching by bringing your students insights about recent discoveries and
  strategies for conducting research?
- Which aspects of your teaching could bring a new dimension to
  your research by helping you become a better mentor to other
  researchers or provide you with improved ways of disseminating
  your results?
- Are there connections you can make between these activities and
  your service projects, perhaps by assigning a class a community
  service learning exercise or by performing some community-based
  research?

Finding ways in which your professional activities enhance one another
instead of becoming distractions from whatever you regard as your "real
work" is a step toward better time management, stress reduction, and
improved professional achievement.

6

ENGAGING IN
MEANINGFUL SERVICE

Service sometimes appears to be the forgotten component in the traditional academic triad of teaching, research, and service. Many colleges and universities have centers for excellence in teaching and entire divisions of research but do little when it comes to defining, developing, and rewarding service. Awards for outstanding teaching and research are common. Awards for outstanding service are relatively rare. Even when they do occur, they are often intended primarily for staff and not faculty members. A great deal of attention is paid to teaching and research in faculty development programs, but where do you go to learn how to run a committee meeting effectively, edit a journal, serve as an officer in a professional organization, run for the faculty senate, or chair a search committee? The answer, in too many cases, is that college professors are just supposed to pick up these skills as they go along.

That's not an effective way of promoting meaningful service. As a result, it's useful to have the following tools in your professional toolkit as you build your career as a college professor.

1. **Familiarity with parliamentary procedure.** The vast majority of committees in higher education run in accordance with the guidelines for parliamentary procedure outlined in such works as

Robert and Patnode (1989) and Robert and Robert (1990). But there is widespread misunderstanding about the specific rules delineated in these works (See Buller, 2014). Just becoming familiar with such issues as how and when to make a proper motion, which motions must be seconded, which motions may be debated, and how votes must be conducted is itself a meaningful contribution to service. You can help committee meetings run much more effectively and begin establishing your reputation as a good chair and parliamentarian.

2. **Familiarity with your institution's unique committee structure.** There is no single structure that suits the way in which every college and university is organized. Particularly if you worked at another institution before taking your current job, you may assume that the responsibilities assigned to the departmental personnel committee, college curriculum committee, and faculty senate at your former school are identical to those assigned to similar groups where you are now. In the same way, there may be groups at your institution with names that don't always reveal their precise function. (What does the academic affairs committee do, for example, and how do its responsibilities differ from those of the program advisory committee?) Understanding the precise duties and operations of the various committees at your current institution will help you become more intentional about your service and less burdened by responsibilities that interfere with your goals in teaching and research.

3. **Familiarity with the way in which official positions are assigned in your professional organizations.** Another important service contribution consists of those activities we engage in, not simply for our own academic units but for our disciplines as a whole. For example, working on the program committee for a conference exposes you to what other professionals in your field are doing and gives you insight into how to write proposals that have a greater likelihood of being accepted. In much the same way, serving as a reviewer for a funding organization provides you with an inside look into how decisions about awarding grants are made. Chairing a session at a conference or serving as an officer in an organization benefits your own institution by making it clear that faculty members who work there are making important contributions on a regional, national, or international level.

CASE STUDY 6.1: MEETING EXPECTATIONS

As a new tenure-track assistant professor at Substandard State University, you had very little idea of what meetings of the Policy and Review Committee (PRC) would be like. No matter how low your expectations were, however, the first meeting you attended failed to live up to them. Your dean recently appointed you to this college-wide committee by sending you a letter specifying that the term of your appointment would be three years but failing to mention anything at all about what the PRC actually did or why you were selected for it. You tried asking a few senior members of your department, but they were nowhere to be found when you stopped by their offices nor did they answer the email you sent them. You also did a search of your institution's website, but you couldn't find any descriptions of the tasks performed by this committee. All you knew when you went to your first meeting was that it was scheduled for 2:00 p.m. Tuesday in Room 301 of Old Main and that you were expected to be there.

A little after 2:10 that Tuesday afternoon, Dr. Cavalier R. Rash, a tenured full professor who's served for many years as chair of the PRC, arrives, notes that four of the group's thirty-eight members are present (including both Dr. Rash and yourself), and starts the meeting. "I suppose we may as well get under way," Dr. Rash begins. "Does anyone have any business for the Policy and Review Committee today?" You're about to say that, because you're new to the group, you'd really like an overview of the PRC's responsibilities when another member, Dr. Mousie Diffident, tentatively raises a hand.

"Um, I do have that proposal from the Subcommittee on Procrastination," Dr. Diffident begins, speaking in a voice so quiet that you can barely make out the words. "We've been working on it for a couple of months and just finished our recommendation last week. So, I'd like to suggest that we take that up."

"Is there a second?" Dr. Rash asks. A few moments of awkward silence pass. You're reluctant to second the motion yourself since you're so new to the committee and uncertain about what the recommendation says and even about the purpose of the committee itself. Dr. Rash continues, "Well, you know I can't vote since I'm *ex officio*. Anyone? Anyone at all?" Since no one says anything, Dr. Rash concludes, "Well, I guess it dies for lack of a second. Better luck next time, Mousie. Is there any other business?"

The fourth member in attendance, Dr. Pompous B. Strident, then speaks up. "I had a really hard time finding a parking place for this meeting. I'd like to move that all members of the PRC who've been on the committee for five years or so be given a dedicated parking spot in front of the building."

"Finally, a good idea," Dr. Rash adds. "Is there a second?" Another few awkward moments of silence go by until finally Dr. Rash goes on, "Seriously? No one's going to second this great idea?"

"Um, I guess I could maybe second the motion," Dr. Diffident says rather hesitantly.

"Okay, it's been moved and seconded that everyone who's served on the PRC for about five years get a dedicated parking spot with his or her name on it in front of Old Main," Dr. Rash says. "So, that's now approved. Any more business? No? Move to adjourn. We vote with our feet," Dr. Rash says, bolting from the chair and leaving the room before you even had a chance to ask, "What just happened here?"

Questions

1. What violations of standard parliamentary procedure occurred at this meeting?
2. What occurred that, although it might not technically be a violation of parliamentary procedure, wasn't conducted in an effective or appropriate manner?
3. What could each of the following people or groups have done differently so as to make this committee (or at least this particular meeting of the committee) more effective?
   a. The institution
   b. Your dean
   c. Dr. Rash
   d. The other members of the PRC
   e. The other members of the PRC who attended the meeting
   f. You
4. In the scenario, you are described as a tenure-track assistant professor while the committee chair is a tenured full professor. Given this status differential, is there anything you can do to help the PRC function more effectively?

Resolution

Even though the situation described in this case study is a bit extreme, the inefficient and unprofessional way in which this committee operates is encountered from time to time even at the most prestigious colleges and universities. Particularly for bodies on which chairs can serve for an extended period of time, committees sometimes become the private fiefdoms of these faculty members and adherence to the rules of parliamentary procedure become lax. Violations of standard operating procedures for this committee include the following.

- Only four of the committee's thirty-eight members were in attendance at the meeting. Although there is no set number or percentage of members who must be present in order to form a quorum—the rules governing what constitutes a committee's quorum should be established in its bylaws or operating procedures—it's highly unlikely that such a small group would meet the criterion set. If the chair or any other member received proxy votes from those who couldn't attend, that should have been made clear. As a result, the actions taken during this committee meeting are unlikely to be valid.
- Despite the chair's action, a report or recommendation from a subcommittee doesn't require a second. Since that report or recommendation comes from more than one person, it is considered to be automatically seconded by others on the subcommittee who voted in favor of it.
- Dr. Rash appears to misunderstand the meaning of the term *ex officio*. It means that a person serves on the committee by virtue of a position that he or she holds. It has nothing to do with voting rights. For example, a department chair may be an *ex officio* member of a curriculum committee as specified by that department's bylaws. Unless those bylaws explicitly state that the chair is a non-voting *ex officio* member of the committee, he or she is entitled to vote like any other member.
- Dr. Rash also seems to misunderstand how committees make decisions. Matters aren't resolved once there is a motion and a second. Those actions only *initiate* debate; they don't conclude it. The discussion should then culminate in a vote, withdrawal of the motion, or a decision to table discussion until a later date.

- Although motions to adjourn should not be debated, they need to be seconded and voted on like any other motion.

In addition, there are several things people do that, although not technically violations of formal procedures, certainly fall far short of accepted best practices.

- The purpose and composition of the committee were very hard for you to find. If the function of a committee is not described in a publicly posted set of bylaws, this information should be available to members, prospective members, and other interested parties either online or in a frequently updated handbook.
- A committee's name ought to provide at least some indication of its function. It's unclear from this committee's name what types of policy it's involved in and what sorts of issues it reviews.
- The chair arrived late for the meeting. While punctuality should be the goal of every member, it's particularly important that the person convening the group be on time. That need increases even more for meetings when new members are joining the group and may wish to be briefed about the issues under consideration.
- Not only was an agenda not distributed in advance of the meeting (so that the members could come prepared to discuss the various items under consideration), but there was no printed agenda at all. The chair failed even to provide an oral agenda at the start of the meeting.
- Since the responsibilities of the committee are unclear, it is impossible to know whether Dr. Strident's motion about parking falls within the PRC's purview. In any case, most universities regard parking policy as falling within the administration's sphere of authority, not the faculty's. A committee can't just vote on issues unrelated to its responsibilities.
- Although Dr. Rash deferred from voting or commenting on Dr. Diffident's committee report, using the position of chair as an excuse for doing so, that pretext falls away when Dr. Strident makes a motion. In that case, Dr. Rash's opinion of the issue becomes very clear, and the discussion is one-sided as a result. Similarly, although claiming not even to be able to second or vote on Dr. Diffident's

motion, Dr. Rash feels perfectly comfortable moving to adjourn, an
action that should come from the members, not the chair.

- Dr. Diffident doesn't really second Dr. Strident's motion. Seconds
  should be clear and unambiguous.

As a result of these poor practices, you approach the dean about the
possibility of serving as your college's parliamentarian. The dean likes
this idea and appoints you to the position. While doing so is a struggle at
times, you work over the next four years professionalizing the meetings
conducted at the university. Your service becomes so widely recognized
that, a short time afterward, you leave Substandard State University to
accept a position as dean of the College of Highly Professional Procedures at Exemplary International University.

DOES SERVICE REALLY MATTER?

The degree of importance that different institutions assign to service
varies considerably from institution to institution. In their survey of
faculty members, the authors asked respondents to indicate, on a slid-
ing scale of 0 percent to 100 percent, how much weight was assigned to
service when various types of personnel decisions (renewal of contact,
promotion and tenure, merit increases, and the like) were being made.
The answers ranged from 5 percent to 60 percent, with the average
being 26.92 percent and the median being 20 percent. In general, community colleges tended to place the greatest amount of emphasis on
service when faculty members were being reviewed, research universities the least.

Similarly, when respondents were asked what percentage of committee work they regarded as *valuable* at their institutions (as opposed to a
waste of the committee members' time), answers ranged from a low of
5 percent to a high of 90 percent, with the average being 39.92 percent
and the median being 37 percent. To put it another way, college professors tend to think that roughly two-thirds of the time they spend doing
committee work would be better devoted elsewhere.

The number of committees the average untenured faculty member
serves on ranged from one to eight(!) in the responses received to the

survey, with the average being 2.9 and the median being 2. For tenured faculty members, the number of committees ranged from one to seven, with the average being 3.7 and the median being 3. This result suggests that, despite the common belief that faculty members allow themselves to be overburdened with committee work until they receive tenure and shirk their responsibilities thereafter, the opposite actually appears to be true: Senior faculty members tend to be even more engaged in institutional service than are their junior colleagues.

The authors' survey then asked whether it was currently possible at the respondent's institution for a faculty member to earn promotion from assistant to associate professor based largely on the quality of his or her service. Most, 84.6 percent, said no, 11.6 percent said yes, and 3.8 percent gave other answers, such as "In theory promotion must be based on exemplary teaching and exemplary work in either scholarship or service. In actual practice, however, promotion based largely on service rarely, if ever, occurs."

The result was much the same when later promotions were considered. When asked whether it was currently possible at the respondent's institution for a faculty member to earn promotion from associate to full professor based largely on the quality of his or her service, 80.7 percent said no, 15.3 percent said yes, and 4 percent gave other answers, again citing such factors as an inconsistency between what institutional policies say and how they are actually interpreted. As one respondent put it, "Promotion based largely on service happens very rarely at our school, but it does happen."

Although the difference is not great, it's somewhat surprising to see that it's slightly more common for faculty members to be promoted to the rank of full professor than to associate professor. Common wisdom at most institutions holds that increased scholarship is what distinguishes the professor from those holding other ranks. At certain schools, at least, high levels of scholarship may not be the only means to reach this rank, a factor we'll wish to explore further in the next chapter.

The following are a few observations that the faculty members who answered the survey provided about how much service counted in faculty evaluations at their institutions:

- A growing challenge for us is how to define "regional engagement": Does it count as service or applied research?

- We are a teaching institution. If your teaching is poor, you will never be promoted no matter how exceptional your research or service may be.
- Our institution doesn't have a research requirement. As a result, service is the highest weighted factor.
- Research and teaching remain the coin of the realm throughout higher education. Collegiality is beginning to be considered as an evaluative factor, along with service: Both are considered together at our institution under the label of "Citizenship."
- Since our program prepares people for the health professions, service is a large part of our curriculum and departmental values. But it is not regarded as highly elsewhere at the institution.
- For us, a consistent history of excellence is much more important than the weighting of the individual areas.
- Our standards say that an applicant for promotion has to be excellent in all three areas: teaching, service, and scholarship. But in addition to this, the person's service has to be at least satisfactory in each of the following areas: service to the department, college, university, profession, and community. In practice, successful applicants are almost always people who are rated excellent in all those levels of service or perhaps all but one or two.

SCENARIO 6.1

Imagine that an institution has the following committees:

- **Faculty Senate:** Meets every Friday from 2:00 until 5:00 p.m. with a very broad charge that deals with all issues of faculty concern and making policy recommendations to the administration.
- **Curriculum Committee:** Meets monthly to review and approve all new academic programs, courses, and substantive changes to curriculum.
- **E-Learning Committee:** Meets monthly to recommend policies with regard to online programs, provide guidance on e-learning issues to the Curriculum Committee, and approve hardware and software requests directly related to e-learning.

- **Undergraduate Research Forum Committee:** Meets once during
  the fall and three times during the spring to develop, plan, and select
  student participants for the institution's annual Undergraduate Research Forum, which takes place the week prior to commencement.
- **Study Abroad Committee:** Meets as needed to review and approve applications from faculty members who wish to develop new
  study abroad programs.
- **Departmental Personnel Committee:** Meets twice each semester to make recommendations to the chair about issues related to
  personnel decisions (contract renewal, merit increases, tenure, and
  promotion) for each faculty member in a specific discipline.
- **Institutional Promotion and Tenure Committee:** Meets weekly
  throughout the spring to review and make recommendations to the
  provost in the case of each faculty member applying for promotion,
  tenure, or both.
- **Faculty Awards Committee:** Meets once each year to select nine
  faculty members from across the institution who will be recognized
  at a public ceremony for their excellence in one of three areas:
  teaching, research, and service.
- **Institutional Review Board:** Meets twice a month to review proposals for research projects that involve human subjects and determine whether those projects meet required standards.

Imagine, too, that the following faculty members are considering which
committee assignments they ought to pursue:

- **Professor A:** A first-year tenure-track assistant professor fresh out
  of graduate school
- **Professor B:** A third-year tenure-track faculty member who is
  clearly on track for tenure in terms of teaching and research and
  whose passion is classroom teaching
- **Professor C:** A recently promoted and tenured associate professor
  who would like to explore the possibility of an administrative career
- **Professor D:** An award-winning associate professor who has received numerous grants, patents, and citations for excellence in
  research
- **Professor E:** A full professor who is having trouble remaining engaged after many years of, in this faculty member's words, "teaching
  the same thing over and over again"

- **Professor F:** A well-loved senior full professor who is interested in leaving an important legacy

Challenge Question:

Which committee assignment(s) would you recommend that each of these six faculty members pursue?

Scenario Outcome:

You understand that expectations for service contributions are likely to change over the course of a faculty member's career. You also recognize that different service opportunities may be appropriate based on the individual needs or goals of each faculty member. With these principles in mind, you make the following recommendations:

- **Professor A:** Since this faculty member is new to both the profession and the institution, he or she should probably not pursue any committee assignments (since they can occupy time that needs to be devoted to teaching and research) or a committee that requires a fairly small time commitment, like the Undergraduate Research Forum Committee.
- **Professor B:** Since this faculty member is clearly exceeding expectations in teaching and research, several possibilities exist. Professor B could pursue appointment to a highly visible and important committee like the Faculty Senate or Curriculum Committee so that his or her service contributions will be widely known when going up for promotion and tenure in a few years. Alternatively, because of the faculty member's strong interest in teaching, an appointment to the E-Learning Committee or Study Abroad Committee would also be a suitable possibility.
- **Professor C:** Because of this faculty member's interest in considering a future in administrative positions, it would be useful to seek positions on such groups as the Faculty Senate, Departmental Personnel Committee, or Institutional Promotion and Tenure Committee.
- **Professor D:** Due to this professor's strong record of excellence in research, good opportunities would be service on the Undergraduate Research Forum Committee or the Institutional Review Board.

> If, however, the faculty member were trying to balance his or her
> portfolio before applying for the rank of full professor, one of the
> more teaching-oriented committees would also be appropriate.
> - **Professor E:** In order to re-engage this senior faculty member, good
>   options would include the E-Learning Committee (where he or she
>   would be exposed to new platforms for and approaches to pedagogy),
>   the Faculty Awards Committee (where he or she may be inspired by
>   the exciting work that others are doing), or the Institutional Review
>   Board (where he or she may develop new ideas for research).
> - **Professor F:** Since this faculty member is interested in his or her
>   legacy, a truly important committee like the Faculty Senate or
>   Curriculum Committee would be a good choice. Service on the
>   Promotion and Tenure Committee or Faculty Awards Committee
>   would also give this faculty member further exposure to the work of
>   colleagues who will be following in his or her footsteps.

ADVICE ABOUT SERVICE

On their survey of college professors, the authors asked those who replied what advice they would give about service to a faculty member
who was just starting out. Because of the differences in how much
service is valued and rewarded at various institutions, people's answers
were quite diverse. Some respondents emphasized the important role
that service can play in building a career as a college professor.

- Use service as a mechanism for professional enrichment, not simply as a mind-numbing obligation. Seek out service opportunities
  that matter to you and use them to connect with people who are
  outside your department and to exercise some of your gifts that are
  not tapped into when you teach or conduct research.
- Service [at our institution like many others] is mission-driven and
  an expected part of what each faculty member does. You should
  give it a very high priority.
- Take service seriously. Use service to seek out leadership roles.
- Focus your service activities so as to build expertise in particular
  areas and conserve your energy.

- Service is not about amount, but quality. It will help you succeed in personnel decisions if you are on the borderline in either of the other two areas (teaching and research). It is certainly noticed when raises are considered and when you are asking for something. It's always a good idea to be a good departmental citizen because you are more likely to hear yes when you ask for things if you are.
- The service you perform really does matter, and it can pay off to your advantage as a college professor.
- Use your service to provide you with visibility to colleagues in other departments and other colleges.
- If you want to continue your career as a college professor, try to become involved in as many service activities as possible.
- Don't hang back. Reach out and volunteer for service on committees that will put you in contact with people who can tutor you and with units of the institution that will expose you to collaborative opportunities.
- Service is important. It should be seen as valuable tool for promotion and tenure.
- Find a senior faculty mentor to guide you in your service activities.
- Keep careful track of your service and make sure you are providing service at every level of the institution, profession, and community in at least one way. Also, make sure your service activities inform your teaching (or vice versa) and are also connected somehow to your scholarship. Document your participation in your service activities. If an activity is something in which you cannot actively participate, or which is not connected to your teaching, consider deferring it to later when you've received tenure. You don't want to spend a lot of time doing something that could diminish time you spend on other efforts toward tenure.

Other respondents, however, cautioned against allowing service obligations to become distractions from the "more important" faculty functions of teaching and research.

- Keep your service obligations under control. Don't volunteer for every committee you're offered. Service eats up research time and doesn't count for very much in the reward structure.

- Don't overcommit to service at the expense of the quality of your teaching.
- Try to be mentored by a senior faculty member regarding which service opportunities are better. Some committees are very labor intensive (stay away from these) while others have high profile (pursue these).
- Publish like there is no tomorrow. Service can come later.
- Perform only minimal service except to your unit and profession until you're tenured.
- Don't be afraid to say no when offered a chance to be on a committee. Most junior faculty members do not wish to offend their senior colleagues or administrators who ask them to get involved in a committee that will take much time away from their teaching, research, and home life. So I always recommend that new faculty members adhere to the following script: "I would love to help you, but I need to check my calendar. I have a number of research projects under way, and I'm trying some new things in my courses to get the students more engaged in active learning. So I'm not sure off the top of my head if I can fit this in."
- Choose wisely. Always try to find service projects that really matter. Negotiate service options with your chair, particularly if first-year faculty members have an opportunity to be protected from service obligations.
- Follow the tenure and promotion guidelines to the letter and adhere to those criteria as you plan out your years on tenure track.
- Keep your service commitments limited, but be visible to your colleagues.

What should we conclude from advice that seems so contradictory? Perhaps the wisest course for new faculty members is to talk to their chair, dean, or a trusted mentor about the role that service plays in their program and which types of service activities they will be expected to perform. What is true for one institution may not at all be true at another, and you can't always assume that what worked for your colleagues in other programs will be the best approach you can take in your own career.

SCENARIO 6.2

Imagine that you're advising a faculty member in his or her second year at your institution. If your school offers tenure, imagine that this faculty member holds a tenure-track appointment. If your school doesn't offer tenure, think in terms of your institution's reward structure: Which activities tend to contribute most to a person's career?

The faculty member has an opportunity to engage in the following service activities:

- The department's library committee, a group that meets only infrequently to recommend which information resources the school's library should acquire in the department's discipline
- A search committee for a new provost
- An outreach effort to help disadvantaged students at a local high school become better prepared for college
- The program committee of the national professional organization in the faculty member's discipline
- Membership in the local Rotary Club
- Faculty secretary for the college where the sole duty is to take minutes at monthly meetings of the college's faculty
- Union representative for the discipline
- A site reviewer for the school's major accrediting body

Challenge Question:

Which of these activities would you encourage the faculty member to pursue and which of them would you encourage the faculty member to defer?

Scenario Outcome:

Since this scenario is based on your own institution, your answer is likely to be different from that of readers who work at a different kind of institution. For example, at some schools community service, such as the outreach program to the local high school and membership in the Rotary Club, isn't considered service at all: The types of service that are rewarded and recognized are limited to actions performed on behalf of the institution or the faculty member's own discipline. At other schools, community outreach is a significant component of the school's mission.

In general, however, faculty members early in their careers should probably focus on service activities that give them the highest visibility with the least time commitment. In the scenario above, these activities include service as the faculty secretary of the college, membership in the program committee of the faculty member's professional organization, and work as a site reviewer for the institution's accrediting body. Serving on the search committee for a new provost or as a union representative is probably too politically charged and time-consuming for junior faculty members.

SCENARIO 6.3

Imagine the same scenario as above except that the person you're advising is an associate professor (with tenure, if your institution offers it) who hopes to become a full professor at the earliest opportunity.

Challenge Question:

Which of the activities bulleted above would you encourage the faculty member to pursue and which of them would you encourage the faculty member to defer?

Scenario Outcome:

Since this faculty member is at a different stage of his or her career, you'll probably make different recommendations than those you made for the junior faculty member above. In this case, work as the college's faculty secretary or service on the department's library committee is unlikely to be of much value in helping advance this faculty member's career goals. Those activities may still be very useful to the institution, but our concern in this scenario is getting the faculty member promoted. In much the same way, membership in the Rotary Club and volunteering at a local high school may be noble activities, but they're unlikely to be of much value when this faculty member applies for promotion.

Unless the institution is operating in such a politically charged environment that only full professors should hold these posts, serving on the provost's search committee or as a union representative may be precisely the right choices to provide institution-wide exposure to the faculty member at this stage of his or her career.

DEVELOPING A PHILOSOPHY OF SERVICE

We tend to be familiar in higher education with formal statements of a faculty member's philosophy of teaching or research. These statements help us put our achievements into context, explaining not just *what* we did but also *why* we did it. They also help promotion and tenure committees see us as a complete person, not merely a series of accomplishments on a résumé.

Statements of one's philosophy of service are far less common, but they can be equally important for you as well as others. Thinking through your philosophy of *why* you serve, *whom* you serve, and *how* you serve can cause you to become more intentional and effective in seeking meaningful service opportunities. It can also inform others why (just to choose an example) you may have thought it best to perform service for your institution's regional accrediting body rather than your major disciplinary organization or why you have led more departmental committees than college committees.

A good statement of service philosophy should be relatively short (around one hundred words), reflect your core principles, and be in alignment with the choices you've actually made in your service opportunities. Since first-person forms (I, me, my) can get rather repetitive and seem self-congratulatory in a philosophy statement, it's often best to write these statements in the third person.

The following is an example of what a philosophy of service statement might look like:

Higher education is best viewed as a service profession. Much as Ernest Boyer redefined scholarship in *Scholarship Reconsidered* (1997) and

Richard Keeling and Gwendolyn Dungy redefined teaching in *Learning Reconsidered* (2004), it is time for college professors to re-examine service in a movement that might be called *Service Reconsidered*. Everything we do in academic life is service. Teaching is service to our students. Scholarship is service to our profession. What universities generally term "service" consists merely of contributions made for the greater good of one's institution, discipline, and community. Thus, by using their professional talents to serve those who teach, learn, and perform research, college professors take their contributions to a new level: improving themselves by working for others while improving the quality of academic life by serving the needs of their students and colleagues.

Naturally your own philosophy statement will reflect your individual values and be expressed in language that best suits your personality. You may wish to include your philosophy of service (as well as your philosophy of teaching and research) at appropriate points in your *curriculum vitae*. Those statements provide useful introductions for anyone who reads your materials and needs to make a personnel decision based on your work.

CASE STUDY 6.2: SERVING ALL THE WAY TO UNEMPLOYMENT?

One day your supervisor asks you to mentor a colleague. "I think Dr. Scrupulous can use some candid advice. We have time to solve this problem, but we're going to need to address it right away." Dr. Scrupulous is a faculty member in your discipline who has now served in a tenure-track position for three years. Both student and peer evaluations of Dr. Scrupulous's teaching have been very positive, and several of Dr. Scrupulous's students at both the undergraduate and graduate levels have presented their research at national conferences.

The problem, as your supervisor sees it, is Dr. Scrupulous's service—not the lack of it, but rather the huge amount of it. Dr. Scrupulous has been devoting so many hours to community service that there has been little progress in research. Since joining the faculty, Dr. Scrupulous has published only two refereed articles in second-tier journals, and one of those articles was as second author. Dr. Scrupulous has never applied for a grant or engaged in any other activity that your discipline traditionally regards as research. Instead, Dr. Scrupulous devotes more than twenty hours each week to what your chair describes as "community service projects" and, in fact, contributed all of last summer to this work.

"We've got to get Dr. Scrupulous to develop a better balance in teaching, research, and service. Right now, there's been exceptional work in teaching and community service (though less of a contribution to institutional or disciplinary service) and very little progress in research. At this rate, I can't foresee a positive tenure decision in three years. Can you help?"

You agree that, at the very least, you'll try to help out your colleague and ask Dr. Scrupulous to join you for an informal conversation the following day. You meet off-campus at a quiet café, exchange a few pleasantries, and then gradually move into why you've asked for this meeting. You explain how important it is to develop a balanced portfolio of teaching, research, and service, speak favorably of Dr. Scrupulous's work in the classroom and community, and end by noting that your supervisor is concerned about the record of research—or lack thereof—that Dr. Scrupulous is amassing.

Dr. Scrupulous listens politely and then responds, "You know, I've had this conversation with our supervisor several times, and I don't know why my ideas just aren't getting through. You see, for my specialty, service *is* my research. I perform the type of scholarship that's known as Community-Based Participatory Action Research or CBPAR. It's an outgrowth of community service learning that takes those approaches into some really interesting and innovative directions.

"What we do is partner with community members and representatives of community action on a research project that benefits the stakeholders and to which we all contribute our expertise, voice in decision making, and ownership of the results. For instance, if I were conducting research into effective strategies for drug rehabilitation, I might want to start by gathering some baseline data on community drug use. But the data that I'd collect myself would be worthless: People in the community would see me as an outsider, an academic, and maybe even connected with law enforcement. They'd tell me what they think the authorities want to hear, not their own experience with drug use.

"But if I work in a partnership with community members who collect the data, the information they get is likely to be much more reliable: People trust those whom they know from the community, and we'd have better baseline data to help us decide what interventions work and thus better serve the community. What I do is apply this kind of approach to projects in our discipline. It's just the kind of innovative research that our institution always says it stands for.

"That division of academic work into teaching, research, and service is now rather dated. My service and research are inseparable from my teaching. It's through engaging students directly in cutting-edge research that wins me those great student and peer evaluations and gets our students invitations to present their findings at national conferences. Similarly, those hours I spend in service are really spent in community service, community-based research, and community service teaching. For what I do, there's no clear dividing line. Can you help me explain that to our supervisor?"

Questions

1. What do you do?
   a. How do respond to your supervisor who asked you to help solve a problem?
   b. How do respond to Dr. Scrupulous who asked you to explain CBPAR to your supervisor?
2. Would your response be different if any of the following were true?
   a. If, instead of being in the third year of a tenure-track position, Dr. Scrupulous were going up for promotion and tenure this year.
   b. If, in response to your explanation of CPBAR, your supervisor's response were, "Look: I'm old-fashioned. That kind of stuff just isn't research in my book. To me, research consists of peer-reviewed publications and externally funded grants. Period. Tell Dr. Scrupulous that I'm not going to give a positive tenure recommendation unless I see a whole lot more traditional research, not this touchy-feely social engagement nonsense."
   c. If, after talking to Dr. Scrupulous, you recognized that some of your own scholarship could be regarded as Community-Based Participatory Action Research.

     d. If your institution's guidelines for promotion mention service to the department, college, institution, and discipline but say nothing at all about whether community service counted for personnel decisions.

3. At the institution where you work, could Dr. Scrupulous present a compelling case for excellence in research by pointing to the way in which he or she mentored students in effective strategies for conducting their own research?

4. Can you think of any other activities that blend teaching, research, and service into a single pursuit in the way that CBPAR does?

5. Can you think of scholarly activities in your own discipline that some faculty members would recognize as rigorous research while others might dismiss them as unworthy of being recognized as appropriate research for a college professor?

Resolution

You conclude that, if Dr. Scrupulous is going to be successful when applying for tenure and promotion, a multipronged strategy will be necessary. First, you suggest that Dr. Scrupulous write a philosophy of service statement that outlines what CBPAR is and that is accompanied by similar statements on the philosophy of teaching and research. You suggest that these three statements be included in Dr. Scrupulous's curriculum vitae as a way of placing the faculty member's achievements into a clearer context.

Second, you recommend that Dr. Scrupulous begin educating the institutional community on the nature of CBPAR. You recommend discussions of this approach at faculty meetings, a public lecture to which campus administrators are invited, and several open forums at which students and faculty members discuss the impact of their own work in Community-Based Participatory Action Research.

Third, since your supervisor regards grants as an appropriate form of research in your field, you encourage Dr. Scrupulous to apply for external funding to support this form of scholarship. You note that receiving a grant from outside the institution will provide a sort of professional validation that the work Dr. Scrupulous is doing really is research and is recognized as such by authorities in the discipline. By making these

suggestions, you believe that you're fulfilling both your supervisor's request to solve the "problem" of Dr. Scrupulous's lack of "research" and
your colleague's request to help explain the nature of CBPAR to your
supervisor.

FOR REFLECTION

Of all the activities that college professors engage in, service is perhaps
the hardest about which to provide general guidelines with regard to
what constitutes excellence and sufficiency. We may find it hard to define excellence in teaching and research, but most of us could agree on
recognizing it when we see it. Service isn't like that. A level of service
that seems excessive at one institution may be regarded as barely sufficient at another. Some schools expect a faculty member to serve on a
committee or task force every now and then. Others expect each faculty
member to serve on three or more each year. Your best guide in terms
of what's appropriate at your institution is to be found in your program's
bylaws and policy manual, the advice you receive from senior members
of your discipline, and the track record established by other successful
faculty members in your field.

7

APPLYING FOR PROMOTION AND TENURE

Few other professional activities fill college professors with as much anxiety and dread as applying for promotion and tenure. So much is at stake: your status, your income, even your ability to continue in your profession. And many aspects of the process are out of your hands. You can work day and night to put together an impressive portfolio, but ultimately it'll be up to others to decide whether it's impressive *enough*. Perhaps the most important lesson for any faculty member who's applying for promotion and tenure to learn is that the human element in the process is something to take into consideration but not something to blow out of proportion.

Three basic principles should guide you in your application for promotion and tenure.

1. **You have to earn it.** No one receives tenure and gets promoted simply for being a nice person or doing the bare minimum of the job. Tenure and promotion are rewards for exceptional work, not entitlements for assigned work. Try to find out what the portfolios of recent successful candidates looked like. What sort of teaching evaluations did they receive? What was their record of publications, performances, grants, or patents? What type of service did

they perform and how much of it did they perform each year? This information gives you some baseline information about what has been regarded as acceptable in the past. Your goal should then be to break these achievements down into a term-by-term plan from now until you go up for promotion and tenure, fulfill all the items on your plan, and then *exceed* it. The goal should be to not merely do what others have done, but so much more that people who review your materials will have no question at all that you deserve a positive recommendation.

2. **You have to make your case.** Merely meeting your own high expectations isn't enough. You also have to convince other people that you've met—in fact, gone far beyond—the standards set by your institution. It's at this level of the process where the human element enters into promotion and tenure. You may have amassed achievements that are impressive by comparison to anyone else who has ever applied for promotion and tenure at your institution. But if you don't present your materials in a form that persuades other people, your application may well not be successful. Make it as easy as possible for people to say yes to you. Structure your materials precisely as the guidelines indicate. Provide every document required. Keep your dossier neat, well ordered, and easy to review. Your application materials should tell a story, and that story should be that you're a faculty member who is unquestionably deserving of promotion and tenure.

3. **The process is rarely as politicized as some people think it is.** You may be told that promotion and tenure at your institution is just a political game. It all depends on whom the dean (or provost or president) likes, who's said the right things to the right people, and who's taken the "right" side on various hot-button issues. While any complex human project is likely to have a political dimension, it's easy to exaggerate the role that politics plays in most promotion and tenure decisions.

4. **You're best defense against a highly politicized process is an excellent portfolio**. Where politics (or at least some degree of subjective human judgment) tends to play a role is in situations where a candidate's application is on the borderline of acceptability. It's much harder to reject a superb application, even if you can't stand the person who submitted it, since the person has

earned promotion and tenure and made a compelling case for it. For this reason, wise college professors devote their "worry time" to amassing achievements and documenting them effectively, not to wondering whether they'll be rejected because political forces are aligned against them.

CASE STUDY 7.1: ALL THAT GLITTERS?

You're a tenured full professor who serves, along with two colleagues, on the Department Evaluation Council (DEC), the group that recommends to the chair which faculty members should be considered for merit increases, promotion, and tenure. The DEC is a very important committee in your department—members must receive approval from at least two-thirds of the faculty in order to be elected—and you take your responsibilities very seriously.

This year, the DEC has only one case to consider: the application of Dee Siever for tenure and promotion to the rank of associate professor. Faculty members at your institution usually go up for tenure and promotion during their sixth year, but Dr. Siever has been encouraged to apply a year early because she's won a number of teaching awards, including "Outstanding University Teaching Professor of the Year" for the last two years. When you receive Dr. Siever's materials, the first thing that surprises you is that it contains no peer evaluations of teaching from the department. In fact, the only letter in support of Dr. Siever's teaching that is not from a student is a glowing evaluation submitted by Dr. Crony, a member of a different department in your college.

The surprises don't end there, however. You wince when you look at Dr. Siever's record of research. It consists of only three brief articles, none of which appeared in peer-reviewed journals. In fact, the articles were all in the same journal, a mediocre online publication that, you discover, accepts virtually everything submitted to it. And then comes the next shock: Dr. Siever's co-author on each article is the same person—Dr. Crony.

The rest of Dr. Siever's materials look equally unimpressive. She indicates that she's "almost completed" another article and notes that it will be submitted to "a prestigious journal" but doesn't tell you which journal. She has served on seven committees each semester, far more than you would have recommended her to take on if you had been her mentor. On the other hand, the chair of Paperwork Elimination Committee did submit a note—ironically on paper—that Dee is always present for their meetings and has contributed greatly to the group's overall effort.

The vast majority of Dr. Siever's portfolio consists of student evaluations of her teaching and thank-you notes from grateful students. Even though faculty members aren't required to do so, Dr. Siever has included every student evaluation of her teaching for each semester and course she has taught. Comments on these evaluations are uniformly positive. You note that typical observations include the following.

- "I *love* this class!!!!!!"
- "Dr. Siever is the best professor I have ever had."
- "Dee is great!"
- "I really liked her class. She is *so* funny. I love her stories."
- "Dee was always there for me."
- "Doc's the best!"
- "We have such a great time in class. I'd take all my classes with Dr. Siever if I could!"
- "Dr. Siever has given me a great deal of confidence. I never had such good grades before this class."

At the first meeting of the DEC scheduled to discuss Dr. Siever's application, you are getting ready to mention some of your concerns when one of the other members, Dr. Columbo, begins to pass out some papers. "I took the liberty of having the provost's office run grade reports on Dr. Siever's classes," Dr. Columbo says. "And I think you'll be interested in seeing what I discovered. She gave every single student in each class either an A minus, an A, or an A plus."

"The university doesn't give A pluses," says Dr. Obvious, the third member of the DEC, says while scanning down the list of grades.

"Exactly," Dr. Columbo continues. "The university doesn't record plus or minus grades of any kind."

"That means . . . " Dr. Obvious says, as the implications of this information begin to become clear.

"You got it," Dr. Columbo interrupts. "Every student in every class that Dr. Siever taught since she came here got an A: Every . . . last . . . one."

You whistle in amazement. "I've seen some high graders before, but nothing like this."

"None of us has seen it," Dr. Columbo adds. "According to the provost's office, it's never happened before."

"Wow," Dr. Obvious says, "I think I'm beginning to understand those stellar student course evaluations."

"Oh, and one more thing," Dr. Columbo adds, as you're all still processing this information. "It seems that many of Dee's classes met jointly with those taught by another professor."

"Another professor?" Dr. Obvious asks. "That can't be right. Any other member of our department would've said something. And the department chair would never stand for it."

"Oh, it wasn't another member of our department," Dr. Columbo says, putting on a well-worn raincoat. "It was Dr. Crony."

Questions

1. Are there any circumstances under which you would still be willing to recommend Dr. Siever for tenure and promotion?
2. What is likely to be the result if you took each of the following actions?
   a. You propose to the DEC that the department not only refuse to recommend Dr. Siever for tenure and promotion but also recommend that her contract not be renewed for the following year.
   b. You recommend that Dr. Siever's application for tenure and promotion be held back this year in order to give her one more year to make a stronger case.
   c. The DEC refers the matter to the department chair without making a recommendation.
   d. You discuss the matter with a representative from human resources.
   e. You discuss the matter with Dr. Siever and ask her to justify her decisions.
3. Would your decision be any different if any of the following were true?
   a. If Dr. Siever were a member of a protected class at your institution.

b. If Dr. Siever were a beloved colleague whom every faculty
member in the department liked.
c. If Dr. Siever were a terrible colleague, and members in the
department had long been hoping to get rid of her.
d. If the institution where this case study took place fell into the
Carnegie classification of Research University with Very High
Research Activity (the old "Research 1" category).
e. If the institution where this case study took place were a community college.
f. If, due to budget cuts, all faculty hiring were frozen, and your
program were likely to lose this position if Dr. Siever did not
receive tenure.
4. Do you believe that the name "Dee Siever" may have caused you
to make any assumptions about this faculty member?

Resolution

You and the other members of the DEC decide that, before you draw
any conclusions, you'll schedule a meeting with Dr. Siever to discuss her
application for tenure and promotion. As soon as the meeting begins,
you mention the committee's concern that every student in her classes
receives an A.

She begins to shift uneasily in her chair. "Yes, I wasn't sure at which
point in this process I should explain that. You see, I have a strong commitment to student success, and so I use an approach called *mastery-based
teaching*. At the beginning of each course, students are given a contract,
and they learn exactly what's required to earn an A, a B, and so on. And
you know our students. The ones who don't want to work hard enough to
get an A drop the class. So, I always end up with all my students planning
to complete A contracts. Then the way the tests and papers work is this:
If students are pursuing an A contract, they retake various versions of an
exam until they merit an A. They're not allowed to take the next quiz or
exam until they do so. You can imagine that, for some of them, this work
backs up quite a bit. I have some students who have a whole lot of quizzes
and exams to complete during the last week of class."

A smile flashes across her face at this memory, and then she continues. "It's the same way with papers. Since the students are all pursuing

A contracts. They have to rewrite them, and then rewrite them again, until I decide that the paper deserves an A. And I'm a very tough grader." She smiles again. "So, by the end of the class, the students who have done terrific work, truly world-class work, get an A plus. Those whose work was excellent, but maybe not world-class, get an A. And those students whose work was simply very, very good get an A minus. Oh, I know the registrar's office doesn't record plus and minus grades, but it motivates the students. And mastery-based teaching is all about finding out what motivates students and then using that to help them succeed. It's terribly time-consuming and perhaps has reduced my research productivity somewhat, but I think it's worth it. As you'll see in this chart I've prepared of the students' later performance, my students then go on to perform at least half a letter grade higher in their subsequent courses than the students who took the same class with anyone else in the department." Dr. Siever blushes when she suddenly realizes that "anyone else in the department" includes you and the two other members of the DEC who are sitting in front of her.

"That all sounds . . . well . . . actually rather brilliant," Dr. Obvious concludes. "Who in the world introduced you to such a technique?"

"Oh, my mentor, Dr. Crony. I'm sorry I don't have a mentor actually in our discipline, but I couldn't find anyone in our department who gave student success the priority I did." Dr. Siever blushes again, but then continues. "Anyway, Dr. Crony and I were forced to publish the initial stages of our research on this technique in a rather undistinguished online journal, I'm afraid. But now that it's proven itself so dramatically, we have this letter of acceptance from a better journal." She reaches into her folder and hands you a letter of acceptance from what anyone in your discipline would clearly regard as the leading journal in your field, a highly selective publication with an acceptance rate of less than 5 percent. The letter from the editor calls their work "groundbreaking" and urges them to continue submitting their manuscripts to the journal. Anyone else in the department would regard it as a major coup to have published in that journal two or three times in an entire career. Now it looks as though Dr. Siever will have published there at least that many times before she's even eligible to be promoted to full professor.

"I know I'm a bit idiosyncratic in my methods. But maybe you'll understand why when you hear my story. My father left my mother when

I was seven and my two sisters were five and three. My mom then had to work two jobs until the youngest one of us was out of high school. It was rough. We never had enough, and I never considered myself college material. Most of my teachers treated me as though they expected me to fail, and I'm afraid I lived up to—or rather down to—those expectations.

"But then when I was in high school, I had this biology teacher who saw something in me. I don't know what. But she believed in me. And she simply wouldn't *let* me fail. If I didn't do well on a test, she'd make me keep studying and retaking it until I understood it all. She was the first person who ever made me feel like I could make something of my life.

"Anyway, when I wanted to go to college, my mother said that she'd help me. She didn't have much, but she said she'd help me. There was only one condition: If I ever got a final grade lower than a B in a course, I'd have to find some other way to pay for college. So, I worked hard and never got a grade lower than a B. In fact, I never even got a B. I had all As in college, and so my professors encouraged me to go on and get my PhD.

"So, here I am. And I'm here *because* that biology teacher and my mother set high standards for me and simply expected that I would reach them. And that's what I see as my calling in life: Finding ways to tell any student who'll listen, 'Look, you can do this, and I'll be with you every step of the way to make sure you do.' I intend to do that for every student I can each day of my career. And, if you'll let me, I'd like to continue doing that here." She paused a moment. "Oh, wait. You were the ones who called this meeting. Is there something you wanted to ask me?"

Now it's your turn to shift uneasily in your chair. "Um, yes, we were just wondering," you begin tentatively, "could you maybe cut back on the committee work a little bit? You're doing so well in teaching and research that we don't want service to get in the way." You and the other members of the committee recommend several improvements Dr. Siever can make to her portfolio so that it presents her case more effectively. You encourage her to write out her philosophy of teaching, include the letter she received from the editor of the prestigious journal she has shown you, describe her research more completely in terms that those who aren't familiar with it would understand, and include a few other supporting documents that will help her make her case.

Dr. Siever assures you that she'll be happy to act on this piece of advice and, after she leaves, the DEC votes unanimously to recommend Dr. Dee Siever for early tenure and promotion.

THE CURRENT STATE OF PROMOTION AND TENURE

In their survey of college professors, the authors asked participants whether their college or university offered tenure for faculty positions. Most, 91.3 percent, of the respondents said yes, and 8.7 percent said no. At all institutions where tenure was not offered, either a multi-year contract or a multi-year, rolling contract was possible.

The survey then asked those who worked at schools that offered tenure whether tenure decisions were linked to promotion (usually to the rank of associate professor) or whether the two decisions were made independently. Fifty-two percent said the two decisions were linked. Forty-eight percent said they were independent.

Although fears about the abolition of tenure are widespread in higher education, relatively few people actually experienced a serious attempt to eliminate it. Of those respondents who worked at institutions that granted tenure, only 4.3 percent said that there had been a serious effort by the upper administration, governing board, or state legislature to abolish tenure at the institution. The other 95.7 percent of respondents said either there had been no such attempt or that they had never heard of one.

What people did experience, however, was an increase in the standards used to make promotion and tenure decisions. Among the survey respondents, 45.4 percent said that expectations for promotion (and tenure, if applicable) had increased somewhat over the past ten years. Fewer, 36.3 percent, said expectations had increased a lot, and 18.1 percent said they were unchanged. No one reported that expectations had decreased.

Those participating in the survey were next asked what percentage of applicants for promotion to any rank got turned down at some point in the process at their institutions. The answers given by college professors averaged 12.64 percent, with a median of 10.25 percent. Those at schools offering tenure were asked a similar question about the rate at which applicants were turned down for tenure at any stage in the process. The average of the answers provided was 8.62 percent, with the median answer being 5 percent.

Participants were asked which of a number of statements regarding promotion they agreed with; they could choose as many as they wanted. In declining order of agreement, the following percentages indicate the number of college professors in the survey who thought the accompanying statements were more true than false:

- 26.7 percent: The system of granting promotion (and tenure, if applicable) at my own institution is basically fair.
- 23.9 percent: At my own institution, we largely have the correct criteria in place for granting promotion (and tenure, if applicable).
- 15.4 percent: Many schools give too much attention to research when granting promotion (and tenure, if applicable).
- 14.0 percent: The system of granting promotion (and tenure, if applicable) across the entire system of higher education is basically fair.
- 8.4 percent: Across the system of higher education generally, we largely have the correct criteria in place for granting promotion (and tenure, if applicable).
- 5.6 percent: The system of granting promotion (and tenure, if applicable) across the entire system of higher education has become highly politicized.
- 2.8 percent: The system of granting promotion (and tenure, if applicable) at my own institution has become highly politicized.
- 2.3 percent: The system of granting promotion and tenure is highly flawed and ought to be revised extensively or replaced.
- 1.4 percent: Many schools give too much attention to teaching when granting promotion (and tenure, if applicable).

SCENARIO 7.1

Three years ago a new president was hired by the governing board with a mandate to transform your institution from a middle-tier teaching institution into a top-ranked research institution. From the very beginning of the new president's tenure, therefore, one message has been loud and clear: Expectations for tenure and promotion are increasing; the level of achievement that was acceptable in the past will no longer be regarded as adequate. Now you're serving on the institution-wide tenure and promotion committee. One of the applications you're reviewing lists relatively few accomplishments in the area of research: only three refereed articles, none of them in very prestigious journals, and one of them with the applicant as third author. In the past, that level of accomplishment would have been regarded as sufficient if the candidate's record of teaching and service were strong enough. Under the new president you're not so sure. In the applicant's cover letter, the following statement appears: "Please remember that I was hired during a period when our school's mission was primarily focused on teaching. I have only had three years to adjust to the new standards, a period not nearly long enough for me to shift my focus. For this reason, I must respectfully point out that I must be evaluated under the standards in place when I was hired, not those in place now." At both the department and college levels, the faculty member's portfolio was recommended for promotion by only a one-vote margin.

Challenge Question:

Now that the portfolio has reached the institutional level, are you more likely to vote in favor of or against this faculty member's application for promotion?

Scenario Outcome:

To begin with, you recognize that administrators at colleges and universities do indeed have the authority to increase standards for tenure and promotion. It happens all the time as institutions change their mission or as expectations throughout higher education nationally develop over time. The key factor, however, is that faculty members must be given adequate time to respond to those increased standards. If the faculty member had only had a few months to adjust his or her scholarly productivity—or if he or she had had the full six years of the probationary period—you believe that your choice would be clear. The issue in this case, in your mind, is whether three years was adequate time for the faculty member to meet the new expectations. Given the close vote at the levels of the departmental and college committees, that seems to be the issue in the minds of others as well.

If your institution doesn't bundle tenure and promotion decisions, one solution might be to split the difference: grant the faculty member tenure (provided, of course, that the record of teaching and service warrants that decision) but withhold promotion until a more impressive record of research can be submitted. If your institution doesn't allow you to separate those two decisions, your choice is harder. You have to make a judgment call on whether a faculty member at your institution could reasonably have been expected to increase his or her research productivity in the time available. The faculty member's field will also be a factor in your decision. In many of the natural sciences, large numbers of short publications are the norm; in these disciplines, three articles would be a very meager output at most institutions. In the humanities, smaller numbers of longer publications tend to be expected; in these fields, it may be appropriate to give a colleague the benefit of the doubt if the articles written to date are of suitable quality.

In the end, therefore, you decide that you do not yet have sufficient information to make a final recommendation. You will present the concerns you have to the other members of the committee, find out more about typical rates of scholarly productivity in the faculty member's discipline, and then vote in accordance with your own conscience and professional standards when you know a bit more.

SCENARIO 7.2

The Department of Strife, Rancor, and Mutual Suspicion has long been a very politicized environment in which to work. It seems as though faculty members are always forming and reconstituting coalitions for or against some cause, administrator, or colleague. As an untenured faculty member in the department at the start of your second year, you find yourself getting conflicting advice. Dr. Mentor, a senior member of the discipline, stops by your office regularly to advise you and strongly recommends that you "get on the right team" as soon as possible. Dr. Dithers, your chair, tells you not to worry about all the infighting and just do your best. You're not sure whether you should trust either piece of advice: Dr. Mentor will be retiring in two years, and Dr. Dithers will soon no longer be chair. Despite Dr. Dithers's calm advice—"Don't worry about any of this. I'll have your back when the time comes."—you know that Dr. Dithers may well not be in a position to do so and may not even be a member of the department's promotion and tenure committee when your application is considered.

Challenge Question:

Who is giving you better advice: Dr. Mentor or Dr. Dithers?

Scenario Outcome:

Even though the "realists" in the department repeatedly say things like "it's not what you know, but it's who you know that gets you ahead here," and "this program is a battlefield, so you have to be tough and take sides in order to survive," you find such sentiments unpersuasive. Even if the Department of Strife, Rancor, and Mutual Suspicion is highly politicized now, that doesn't mean it will remain so in the five years or so before you come up for tenure. New additions like you to the department can be the very people who transform the atmosphere of a program.

One factor that vulnerable faculty members in highly politicized departments often forget is that the department isn't their entire world. There are plenty of other resources—committees at the college and university level, the faculty union (if one exists), administrators, the office of human resources, the faculty senate, and so on—who can provide them with protection if they're unjustly treated by others in their program. With these thoughts in mind, you decide that Dr. Dithers is giving you more practical advice than Dr. Mentor. You're going to avoid political entanglements to the best of your ability, do your job, and amass such an impressive record of achievement that if anyone opposes your application for tenure and promotion in a few years, it will be that person who looks ridiculous, not you.

ADVICE ON APPLYING FOR PROMOTION AND TENURE

The authors' survey of college professors asked respondents, "If you could give one piece of advice to a faculty member who will be applying for tenure and/or promotion within the next few years, what would it be?" The answers fell into several categories. Perhaps the most common type of response was a recommendation to focus on research and publishing, with some participants even urging that these activities take priority over teaching and service. Typical answers included the following:

- Focus on research. Teach as well as you can. And don't let service eat up your time.
- Publish. Publish. Publish.
- Make sure both the quantity and quality of your research are well "above the bar."
- Establish a clear research agenda early and adhere to it.
- Make sure you have a boatload of documented, peer-reviewed research. That seems to be the most important aspect of the promotion process.
- Increase your scholarly activities if you have not yet invested significant amounts of time and effort in this aspect of your responsibilities.

The second most common category of response consisted of those who urged faculty members to pay special attention to their institution's guidelines, make sure that they met those criteria, and carefully document their achievements.

- Know the policies and guidelines for your department, college, and university.
- Be sure you understand what the expectations are and provide concrete evidence in your documentation that you have met those expectations. Tell a story that is convincing.
- Save all the documentation you have and memorize the promotion guidelines.
- Work like you are planning to leave. In other words, pay attention to all the expectations presented in the guidelines and then exceed them.
- Triangulate your data on what it takes to get tenure and promotion at your institution.
- Keep good records so that you can present a well-documented dossier.
- Stick to the guidelines.

A third common category of responses included those that urged future applicants to work closely with a mentor. These responses sometimes also contained advice on knowing and meeting all relevant criteria.

- Meet with a mentor early and often in order to make sure you know what the criteria are and whether you're on track to meet them.
- Get advice from multiple credible sources.
- Know your faculty handbook so that you understand the process. Obtain a mentor to guide you through it, including how to assemble your dossier. And keep excellent written records of your achievements in teaching, research, and service.
- Be mentored by a senior faculty colleague who is familiar with the criteria as well as the politics inherent within the promotion and tenure process.

The remaining responses were more varied. They emphasized such factors as the importance of collegiality, institutional fit, and amassing a strong record of service. In this category were such answers as the following:

- Carefully identify service opportunities.
- Don't forget service to the university.
- Granting tenure is based largely on whether a person fits in or not. If you have to be someone you don't want to be in order to get tenure, then take a job elsewhere. If you love the institution, do your best to show that you are a good fit.
- Make sure your teaching and research are innovative as well as focused.
- Be collegial.

To summarize, therefore, the survey of college professors that was conducted for this book suggested that future applicants for promotion and tenure should seek from the very beginning of their positions to develop a strong record of research, pay close attention to their institution's guidelines, work with a mentor, and demonstrate sufficient collegiality and team spirit that others will view them as a good long-term fit for the institution.

CASE STUDY 7.2: "LEADERS ARE NOT SERVANTS"

After an impressive career at a major research university, you were hired by Upward Trajectory State University as one of a group of scholarly superstars who the upper administration hopes will put it on the national stage for research. You were given almost everything you could want: a salary higher than any you thought you'd ever earn, more startup funding than you knew existed, your own administrative assistant, a large and well-appointed office, and a very light teaching load. The only thing the university couldn't offer you was tenure: According to state law, no one could be hired into a university with tenure; every new professor, regardless of rank, would have to serve at least three years before applying for tenure.

Those three years now have passed, and you've just submitted your application for departmental review. You're not the least bit worried. You have such an enviable record of research, grants, patents, and publications that a person would have to be a fool to vote against you. Besides, from the very day of your interview, you've been treated like the luminary you have every reason to believe you are. Upward Trajectory State University is lucky to have you. You expect the process to conclude quickly, probably result in another massive raise added to your already inflated salary, and a hearty round of applause from your peers—no, that's not right: from your *co-workers*; you *have* no peers.

That's probably why the departmental committee has asked to meet with you this afternoon. They must want to tell you how wonderful your application is—after all, you spent nearly half an hour on it—and to ask whether it can be used as a model for all future applicants to aspire to. As a result, you're a bit confused when the members of the committee spend so much time asking you about your record of service.

"Can you tell us why you never come to department meetings?" one faculty member asks. "And why you told the chair not to appoint you to any committees?"

Fortunately, this question like any other you've been asked in your life is extremely easy to answer. "Oh, well, that sort of thing is really a waste of my valuable time. My charge when I came here was to produce articles for first-tier journals, conduct research, and apply for grants and contracts. All of these activities are very labor intensive, and I've done even more than I was expected to do. Service is . . . well . . . a distraction from my important work. Leaders are not servants. I was hired to lead, not to serve."

"I see," the chair of the committee says. "Well, we'll take those statements into account as we make our decision. You should have our letter within a few days." You leave the meeting, a bit annoyed that no one on the committee thanked you for your time or apologized for inconveniencing you over such a trivial issue. But the members are as good as their word. The very next day you receive a copy of the letter they have prepared for the college committee. In its entirety, it reads as follows.

> The departmental tenure and promotion committee regrets that it cannot recommend the above-named candidate for tenure on the basis of inadequate service and poor collegiality. The vote was nine against the motion to recommend the candidate, with no votes in favor and no abstentions.

"Must be jealous of my research," you conclude. "Time for an appeal to the dean and provost. From the tone of this letter, I'm pretty sure *someone* will lose a job over this issue, and it won't be me."

Questions

1. What is likely to be the result if you did each of the following?
   a. You immediately start to look for another job.
   b. You attend the next departmental faculty meeting and either
      - apologize for the misunderstandings that have occurred, mention that you truly do value your colleagues, and say that you were simply unaware that you were expected to attend these meetings and engage in service; or
      - publicly accuse the members of the departmental committee of engaging in a vendetta against you because of your successful record of scholarship.
   c. You go line by line through your contract, the faculty handbook, and the personnel policies of the office of human resources to see if you can catch either your chair or the members of the departmental committee in a procedural error.
   d. You summon the members of the departmental committee to your office and tell them that, based on the terms of your original appointment, their decision is not acceptable.

e. You hire a labor attorney.

f. You make appointments with the dean, provost, and president to inform them how unjustly you've been treated.

g. You meet with the vice president of development to announce that you will take all of your grants with you if you are forced to leave.

h. You email each member of the governing board a statement complaining about your treatment and indicating everything that Upward Trajectory State University stands to lose if you seek employment elsewhere.

i. You write to the president (with a copy sent to the provost and members of the Board of Trustees) saying that you are a highly successful grant writer and the university is in serious danger of losing you.

2. Would your decision be any different if any or all of the following were true?

a. If you had received the highest student course evaluations of any faculty member in the department.

b. If you and your family were extremely unhappy at Upward Trajectory State University and wish that you had never moved from the prestigious university where you had worked previously.

c. If your spouse had recently served you with divorce papers.

d. If you had planned to retire in three years anyway.

e. If you had recently been recruited for a job by one of Upward Trajectory State University's peer institutions.

Resolution

Insulted by the shabby treatment you received from the departmental committee, you send letters to a number of prestigious universities, letting them know that you'd be available and willing to consider a job offer if it were enticing enough. When none of these letters is answered, you expand your search a bit to a larger pool of universities that, if not uniformly top-tier institutions, are all respectable schools. This batch of letters, too, goes unanswered.

You decide to call a friend at one of these schools to see if you can determine what is going on. "I don't quite know how to tell you this," your friend says, "but the word's gone around about you. Academia's a small world, after all, and if you treat people poorly, people find out. I don't think you've got many supporters left. I mean, I did what I could when your letter came, but no one wants to touch you now with a ten-foot pole."

With your job search at a standstill, you decide to do your best to fight the negative recommendation against your tenure. You soon discover, however, that administrators and faculty committees at other levels of the institution are extremely reluctant to overturn a unanimously negative recommendation at the department level. Your appeals are denied all the way up to the governing board, and you're given one final year on your contract.

You spend this terminal year trying to mend what bridges you can and to find a job at any institution that will take you. After months of searching, you discover that Diploma Mill College, a private, religiously based institution in the upper Midwest, is willing to offer you a job if the indirect costs from your grants will cover their portion of your salary. Taking that job entails a major salary cut and proves to be a humbling experience. Your one consolation is that Diploma Mill's mascot is the crow because that's exactly what you'll be eating until you can put your interrupted career back on track.

CASE STUDY 7.3: WITH FRIENDS LIKE THESE

You are an untenured assistant professor currently in your third year of full-time service at your institution. Having just received the results of your third year probationary review, you realize that you're making good progress toward tenure with just a few areas of difficulty to work on. Your teaching received positive evaluations from students and faculty members alike, you've been actively involved in committee work, and you've received two federally funded grants to support your research. The one major suggestion the review committee gave you was that your publication record might be improved if your data analysis were a bit more sophisticated. The reviewers felt that your research was yielding good results but that you just weren't making the best use of all the data you were gathering from your studies.

One day, you were discussing this concern with Dr. Arnold Benedict, an associate professor in your program. Dr. Benedict says, "That's not a problem at all. I'd be glad to help. Data analysis is kind of my thing. In fact, I think I like that better than all the data gathering and measuring that comes first. Next time you get some information that needs interpreting, let me know, and I'll be glad to give you a hand."

You're pleased by this warm display of collegiality and friendship and so, a few weeks later, you stop by Dr. Benedict's office. "Say, Arnold, remember back when we were talking about that data analysis issue? I've got a huge set now, and it's leaving me at a loss about exactly where to go next. Care to take a look at it?"

Dr. Benedict agrees, and you move your data to a shared drive where he can review it. A few days later, he asks you to stop by because he's got some ideas for you. The resulting conversation goes well, and you find the suggestions he makes to be very helpful. The analyses he's run on the data point out a few correlations you may not have noticed otherwise, and you're quite grateful for such an act of generosity. With Dr. Benedict's help, your publication record does improve, just as the third-year review committee had hoped, and your turn to your friend repeatedly for assistance in the months to come.

The years go by, and you're now in your sixth year, putting some of the final touches on your application for promotion and tenure, which you are confident will meet with approval at each level of the institution. As you're checking the most recent issues of the journals in your field to determine whether any other scholar has cited your work, you notice an article by your friend Dr. Arnold Benedict. "Oh, great!" you think. "Arnold's got something new out, too. Let's see what it says."

As you read the article, you reach a moment where you suddenly feel sick to your stomach. There, in one section of Dr. Benedict's paper, is an analysis of data that you recognize as coming from the information you shared with your "friend." The analysis is far more interesting and sophisticated than anything he ever shared with you. You are positive that he never asked you for permission to use these data or mentioned the conclusions that he drew from them. You scan the author line of the article, the footnotes, the acknowledgments, and anywhere else you can think of: There's no indication whatsoever that the data are yours or that you played any role in this study.

Your "friend" appears not to have had your interests at heart. As you stare at the promotion and tenure application that's nearly complete, you're reminded of who's chairing the departmental committee this year: Dr. Arnold Benedict.

Questions

1. What is likely to be the result if you did each of the following?
   a. You immediately go to Dr. Benedict's office and confront him about stealing your work.
   b. You wait until the next meeting of the departmental faculty and then blindside Dr. Benedict with what you've discovered.
   c. You keep your mouth shut until after a positive decision on tenure and promotion is safely in hand and then contact your institution's committee on research integrity.
   d. You discuss what you've found with your department chair.
   e. You contact a few people outside the department and ask them whether they've ever experienced something similar and, if so, how they responded.
   f. You contact the editor of the journal that published Dr. Benedict's article and lodge an official complaint.
   g. You hire an attorney and bring a suit against Dr. Benedict for intellectual property infringement.
2. Would your decision be any different if any or all of the following were true?
   a. If Dr. Benedict were also your chair.
   b. If Dr. Benedict were an internationally acclaimed scholar in your field with influential contacts at universities all over the world.
   c. If there had been rumblings years before you arrived at the institution that Dr. Benedict's research practices were suspected of being unethical.
   d. If Dr. Benedict had the strong support of every other member of the department while you, as an untenured assistant professor, felt that your position was rather tenuous.

Resolution

You decide that there are several different issues at stake here. First, this problem could not have arisen at a worse time for you personally: You are in the midst of being evaluated for promotion and tenure, and anything that proves to be a distraction for the department—particularly if it involves you—will increase your stress level and potentially have a negative impact on your career. Second, there is a rather serious matter of research integrity involved in your allegations. While you don't recall offering your data to Dr. Benedict for his own use to pay him back for his help with your analysis, you don't feel 100 percent certain that you might not have said something that may have been misconstrued in this way. All in all, you have a mess on your hands that is bad enough if it's Dr. Benedict's mess but that could be disastrous for you if it somehow affects your application for promotion and tenure.

After giving the matter considerable thought, you discuss the matter with your department chair. You've never regarded your chair as particularly effective, and you're especially concerned when the chair's first thoughts are about the negative publicity this incident could bring the program, not the ethics involved or any effect it could have on your career. Finally, after a bit of persuading from you, the chair agrees to file an incident report with the institutional committee on research integrity and make it appear that the chair, and not you, first became suspicious of how Dr. Benedict's data had been gathered.

Predictably Dr. Benedict is outraged when he learns an incident report had been filed against him. He charges into the chair's office and asks, "Why didn't you just come to me and ask me about the data instead of involving an institution-wide committee?" Dr. Benedict claims that you gave him free right to use the data and that he did nothing inappropriate in publishing his observations. He insists that you be brought into the discussion so that you can verify his version of the story. The chair tries to keep you out of it as an untenured member of the department but, at Dr. Benedict's insistence, you're finally summoned to join them.

"Go ahead. Tell our chair," Dr. Benedict begins. "You offered this data to me and told me I could do anything I wanted with it."

The anger on Dr. Benedict's face seems intimidating, but you manage to get out a reply. "If I said that, I only meant you could do whatever you wanted with it to help me analyze it. I never meant you could publish it."

"Oh, so you know about the article?" Dr. Benedict shouts. "Who began this accusation? You or the chair? I just need to know so that my lawyer knows which one of you to sue."

"It doesn't matter who first noticed the article, Arnold," your chair interjects. "It's a public document. The question is, even if you were given permission to use the data, why you didn't acknowledge its source? Why doesn't your junior colleague's name appear even once anywhere in the article?"

The argument between Dr. Benedict and the chair goes on for over an hour. You become increasingly worried that, even in the best-case scenario, the impact of this incident will be that a cloud is cast over your own career. Over the next few months, your application for promotion and tenure and the case against Dr. Arnold Benedict for violations of research integrity both slowly wind their way through the bureaucracy. In the end, your application is successful, but neither you nor anyone else in the program feels like celebrating. Dr. Benedict has a formal letter of censure placed in his file, is denied a merit increase for the year, and otherwise is treated by others as though he had done nothing particularly wrong. He ceases speaking to you, of course, and begins to treat the chair like a personal enemy, but otherwise his career continues as it was before you ever saw his article.

In a sense you've won, although you hardly feel like a winner. You decide that that's what happens in the real world of higher education: There are very few shining heroes and very few outright villains, just a lot of flawed people trying to do their jobs, making mistakes from time to time, suffering the consequences of those mistakes (or not), and trying to put any lessons they learn along the way into their ever-expanding toolkit for college professors.

FOR REFLECTION

Many times college professors ask those who are more experienced for advice on how to be successful when they apply for promotion and tenure. In the authors' experience, there is no guaranteed path for anyone. Promotion and tenure decisions involve an inherently human process of choice and judgment, and any human process will be flawed from time to time. Nevertheless, there are four keys faculty members can use to reach a point at which they're at least in the best position for success when applying for promotion and tenure.

1. **Advice**. Talk to as many people as possible who have been through the process already. What did they do effectively and what would they have done differently? The answers you receive are likely to conflict at times, but certain patterns will emerge if you talk to enough people. Use those patterns to guide you in preparing for

your classes, focusing your research, choosing which committees to serve on, and organizing your materials. Remember that even people who go through the promotion process several times in their careers don't do so frequently: Everyone is dependent on learning from the experience of others.

2. **Fit**. Promotion and tenure decisions are somewhat different in focus. People are promoted on the basis of what they've done; people are tenured on the basis of what they can be expected to do. As such, institutional fit becomes of prime importance in choosing who we want to work with us at a college or university. If you're a world-class scholar but don't seem to be right for the program that's considering you for tenure, you may still get it but your struggle to do so will be significantly harder. Why not make it easier by either fitting in where you are or finding someplace else where you really do fit?

3. **Preparation**. The time to begin understanding the standards and criteria that will be used when personnel decisions are made about you isn't when you're preparing your application. It's the first day on the job. If you don't know now what standards and criteria will be used to determine whether you should be granted tenure and promotion, find out as soon as you can. Develop a clear plan between now and the moment of your evaluation, outlining what you need to do when: How many publications will you need to complete each year? Which committees should you serve on? What scores on student course evaluations are considered appropriate? What level of grant activity will you need to obtain? Give yourself milestones to achieve term-by-term and take those milestones seriously. Your career depends on them.

4. **Collegiality**. People who are respectful, collegial, and civil to students, staff, administrators, and other faculty members put themselves in a much better position to obtain tenure and promotion when they apply. Collegiality is part of the element of fit we discussed earlier. But it's also a matter of the working environment that those who make decisions about you will have. If you had the choice, would you want to work with a collegial faculty member or someone who's difficult to get along with? Even when that question does not affect people's decisions openly, it can color their

outlook subconsciously. It's just as easy to be nice to other people as to treat them rudely, so why not act in a way that is likely to be better for your career?

Remember, too, that, even though you might be the perfect fit for the program and the most collegial faculty member anyone has ever met, lack of achievement in any of the areas for which you're being evaluated could result in an unfavorable decision. As we saw at the beginning of this chapter, you have to *earn* promotion and tenure; no one is simply going to hand it to you.

Moreover, despite the importance of the four keys we just explored, there's nothing you can do to eliminate all the politics from the promotion and tenure decisions made about you. But keep in mind what we saw in this chapter: Your single best defense in overcoming political opposition when you go up for promotion and tenure isn't becoming preoccupied with politics and power struggles; it's amassing an indisputably excellent record of achievement.

EPILOGUE

Our Final Reflections

No book can ever tell you everything you'll need to know about being a college professor. Our skills in the position grow over time through experience and the development of new knowledge. But we've tried in this book to provide you with tools that can make this task, if not easy, then perhaps a little bit easier. In closing, then, we'd like to provide you with a few additional reflections.

- *Be yourself.* It's natural to begin your teaching career by imitating the professors who you believe taught the best when you were a student. It's natural to launch your independent research agenda by imitating the professors you most admired as scholars. But you won't really achieve everything you can as a college professor until your teaching, research, and service all reflect your own individual style. If you're more comfortable with an informal classroom environment, you won't do your best if you mimic the formal style that you associate with one of your own mentors. If you're more comfortable in a more formal, structured learning environment, you won't be at ease if you try to teach like one of your own professors who allowed students to use his or her first name. The goal is not to be like other people, even truly great people. It's to be the best possible version of yourself. And you can't do that if you're hiding behind a mask.

- *Resist cynicism.* Students really do want to learn. It may not seem like it much of the time, but they really do value the contributions we make in helping them achieve their dreams. So, even though it's a common professorial practice to speak slightingly of students, their poor academic preparation, and their slovenly work habits, resist the urge to take this frequent grumbling to heart. One of those students who seems so unpromising right now may someday be your colleague (and that day arrives much sooner than you expect) or an important donor, and the impression you make on them today will stay with them for many years to come.

- *Work with a mentor.* Experienced mentors can pick up where this book leaves off. They can give you advice, help you view situations from alternative perspectives, and offer constructive criticism that will help you improve. Some institutions assign mentors to all new faculty members. At others, you'll have to find your own. In either case, it's important to find someone who's similar enough to you to understand your thought processes but different enough to challenge your assumptions and explore other possibilities. The length of time you work with a mentor will vary according to your needs and what requirements, if any, your institution has. Most new faculty members find working with a mentor for their first year in a position is sufficient. Others prefer to maintain the relationship until they're tenured. Still others find mentors to whom they turn to for advice throughout their entire careers. There's no single path to having a successful relationship with a mentor, but working with one for at least a short period is an experience that most college professors find invaluable.

- *Keep your balance.* Being a college professor can be a 24/7/365 occupation. There's always one more thing you can do to make that next class just a little better, polish that article just a little more, and prepare for that next meeting a little more completely. But just because you *can* do all of that, it doesn't mean that you *should* do all of that. It may seem sometimes that your students will be better off if you put in a few additional hours getting ready to teach. Perhaps they may. But they also may be better off if they have a professor who's living a full, complete, and rounded life, who spends time with his or her family and friends, who keeps up with the news and thus is aware of what's going on in the world, who has appreciation for the breadth of human experience and culture, and who comes to class refreshed because he or she hasn't spent every moment worrying about being sufficiently prepared. Balance is key. Devote time to developing as a great teacher and scholar. But devote time to being a person, too. Your students, research, and colleagues will all be the better for it.

- *Buy your academic regalia.* Particularly if you're just starting out as a college professor, purchasing academic regalia that you'd only use once or twice an academic year may not seem like a very practical expense. But it is one of those professional expenses that helps you become part of the community of scholars. Just as your education and books were professional expenses that you incurred to get where you are now, so does the purchase of professional regalia provide an entrée to the full academic life. By attending commencements, we remind ourselves periodically why we work so hard on behalf of our students. Their successes are a reflection of our successes, and these joyous occasions can help make our more challenging days feel worthwhile. Academic regalia may also be required for other important institutional ceremonies—such as freshman convocation, the inauguration of a new president, and honors awards night—that would make you feel like an outsider if you can't attend them. So, make the investment in a set of regalia of high quality and then use it as often as possible throughout your professorial career.

- *Keep an open mind.* The authors have tried to construct a number of the case studies in this book in such a way that the situation at the end of the exercise looks rather different from the situation at the beginning. Your experience as a college professor is likely to be quite similar. The student who you're certain is just slacking off turns out to be battling a serious illness while simultaneously trying to raise a small child. The faculty member who seemed so gracious to you once turns out to have been merely trying to use you and ends up stabbing you in the back. In an environment as complex as that found in higher education, first impressions aren't uniformly reliable. Keep an open mind and be willing to change your opinion when the evidence warrants.

- *Pay it forward.* Once you feel that you're a full member of the academic community and have gained what you need from your mentors and advisors, it's time to contribute to the development of the next generation of college professors. Become a mentor yourself. Help someone just as someone once helped you. You'll find the experience of contributing to someone else's professional development to be not only rewarding in itself but also a way of continuing your own growth as you crystallize what you've learned about teaching, research, and service in order to convey those lessons to others.

In closing, work as a college professor should be engaging, continually challenging, and fun. That's not to say that there won't be days when your life's made miserable by unmotivated students, stubborn administrators, overly involved parents, mindless paperwork, and an inability to find a decent place to park. Although there are more lucrative careers you might have chosen, we can't imagine a better one.

So remember: The insights you've gained throughout years of preparing for your current role aren't a treasure to be hoarded; they're a set of tools to be used. We hope that this book may have added a few more resources to your professorial toolkit. Now the rest is up to you.

APPENDIX

ATLAS: Academic Training, Leadership & Assessment Services offers training programs, books, and materials dealing with collegiality and positive academic leadership. Its programs include:

- Time Management
- Work-Life Balance
- Conflict Management
- Promoting Teamwork
- Promoting Collegiality
- Communicating Effectively
- Mentoring Faculty Members
- Positive Academic Leadership
- The Essential Academic Dean

- The Essential College Professor
- The Essential Department Chair
- Best Practices in Faculty Evaluation
- Change Leadership in Higher Education

These programs are offered in half-day, full-day, and multi-day formats. ATLAS also offers reduced prices on leadership books and distributes the Collegiality Assessment Matrix (CAM) and Self-Assessment Matrix (S-AM), which allow academic programs to evaluate the collegiality and civility of their faculty members in a consistent, objective, and reliable manner. The monthly ATLAS E-Newsletter addresses a variety of issues related to academic leadership and is sent free to subscribers.

For more information, contact:
ATLAS: Academic Training, Leadership, & Assessment Services
4521 PGA Boulevard, PMB 186
Palm Beach Gardens, FL 33418
800-355-6742; www.atlasleadership.com
Email: questions@atlasleadership.com

REFERENCES

CITED REFERENCES

Adams, D. (1979). *The hitchhiker's guide to the galaxy.* London, UK: Pan Books.

Bean, J. C. (2011). *Engaging ideas: The professor's guide to integrating writing, critical thinking, and active learning in the classroom* (2nd ed.). San Francisco, CA: Jossey-Bass.

Boyer, E. L. (1997). *Scholarship reconsidered: Priorities of the professoriate.* Princeton, NJ: Carnegie Foundation for the Advancement of Teaching

Bransford, J. D., Brown, A. L., Donovan, M. S., & Pellegrino, J. W. (2003). *How people learn: Brain, mind, experience, and school* (8th ed.). Washington, DC: National Academy Press.

Buller, J. L. (Spring 2014). Six myths about conducting effective meetings. *The Department Chair, 24*(4), 16–17.

Chickering, A. W., & Gamson, E. F. (1987). Seven principles for good practice in undergraduate education. *American Association of Higher Education* Bulletin, *39*(7), 3–7.

Coburn, K. L., & Treeger, M. L. (2009). *Letting go: A parents' guide to understanding the college years* (5th ed.). New York, NY: HarperPerennial.

Fink, L. D. (2013). *Creating significant learning experiences: An integrated approach to designing college courses* (Rev. ed.). San Francisco, CA: Jossey-Bass.

Habley, W. R., Bloom, J. L., & Robbins, S. B. (2012). *Increasing persistence: Research-based strategies for college student success.* San Francisco, CA: Jossey-Bass.

Keeling, R. P., & Dungy, G. J. (2004). *Learning reconsidered: A campus-wide focus on the student experience.* Washington, DC: ACPA.

Kuh, G. D., Schuh, J. H., & Whitt, E. J. (1991). *Involving colleges: Successful approaches to fostering student learning and personal development outside the classroom.* San Francisco, CA: Jossey-Bass Publishers.

Robert, H. M., & Patnode, D. (1989). *Robert's rules of order, modern edition.* Uhrichsville, OH: Barbour & Co.

Robert, H. M., & Robert, S. C. (1990). *The Scott, Foresman Robert's rules of order newly revised.* Glenview, IL: Scott, Foresman.

Smith, R. V. (2006). *Where you stand is where you sit: An academic administrator's handbook.* Fayetteville, AK: University of Arkansas Press

Svinicki, M. D., & McKeachie, W. J. (2014). *McKeachie's teaching tips: Strategies, research, and theory for college and university teachers* (14th ed.). Belmont, CA: Wadsworth, Cengage Learning.

OTHER RESOURCES

Bain, K. (2004). *What the best college teachers do.* Cambridge, MA: Harvard University Press.

Barkley, E. F. (2010). *Student engagement techniques: A handbook for college faculty.* San Francisco, CA: Jossey-Bass.

Buller, J. L. (2010). *The essential college professor: A practical guide to an academic career.* San Francisco, CA: Jossey-Bass.

Buller, J. L. (2013). *Positive academic leadership: How to stop putting out fires and begin making a difference.* San Francisco, CA: Jossey-Bass.

Kirk, D. J. (2005). *Taking back the classroom: Tips for the college professor on becoming a more effective teacher.* Des Moines, IA: Tiberius.

Lang, J. M. (2010). *On course: A week-by-week guide to your first semester of college teaching.* Cambridge, MA: Harvard University Press.

ABOUT THE AUTHORS

Jeffrey L. Buller is dean of the Harriet L. Wilkes Honors College at Florida Atlantic University. He holds a doctorate in classics from the University of Wisconsin-Madison. He is the author of ten books on academic leadership, one book on Wagnerian opera, a textbook for first-year college students, twenty-two articles of academic research, 132 articles on higher education administration, and 114 essays and reviews. With Bob, he is a senior partner in ATLAS Leadership Training, which conducts workshops for administrators all over the world, and serves as a consultant to the Ministry of Higher Education in Saudi Arabia in its development of a region-wide Academic Leadership Center.

Robert E. Cipriano is chair and professor emeritus of the Department of Recreation and Leisure Studies at Southern Connecticut State University. He has a doctorate from New York University in Therapeutic recreation, area of concentration in college teaching. He is the author of a book on collegiality in higher education, three textbooks, chapters in three additional textbooks, and more than 160 journal articles. He has been awarded more than $9 million in grants and contracts and delivered in excess of 250 presentations in the United States, Asia, and the Middle East. With Jeff, he is the coauthor of *A Toolkit for Department Chairs* (Rowman and Littlefield, 2015).